When Love Calls

A Memoir of Great Devotion

❦ ❦ ❦

by
Father Norm Supancheck

with
Marcus Brotherton

bird
st.
books

Contents

Overture: *How I Describe Love*   *1*

Chapter 1: *Her Favorite Car*   *11*

Chapter 2: *A Question Rises in Me*   *25*

Chapter 3: *The Road to Serving Others*   *39*

Chapter 4: *What Would We Do?*   *55*

Chapter 5: *Staring at the Sun*   *65*

Chapter 6: *What Have I Gotten Myself Into?*   *79*

Chapter 7: *When I Stopped Panicking*   *93*

Chapter 8: *Facing Death*   *109*

Chapter 9: *Light Streamed through the Window*   *121*

Chapter 10: *How the Years Slip By*   *135*

Chapter 11: *The Worst News Ever*   *145*

Chapter 12: *Where Rose Gardens Once Bloomed*   *159*

Chapter 13: *Something Important about Cars*   *165*

Chapter 14: *Limping, I Continue On*   *173*

Chapter 15: *The Last Gift*   *179*

About the Author   *185*

How I Describe Love

I USED TO DRIVE A TOYOTA PRIUS, one of those eco-friendly hybrids, and I miss the feeling of responsibility it provided, but I'm not looking for any other car than the one I have now. These days I drive a big cream-colored Lincoln Town Car, a strange sort of car for a man in my position to own, yet I drive it with joy and remembrance and tribute. I will hold on tight to this car for as long as I am able.

The Lincoln is not new, even though it looks timeless. It was a gift to me, and given to me used. Fifteen years have passed since it first saw a showroom. It has power windows and locks and bench seats and a CD player and cushioned everything. It reminds me of the wonders of yesteryear, of the promise of eternity, of the protection of Detroit and God. I drive it because of the soul I can still feel surrounding this car. Down the freeways of Los Angeles where I live, this car flies as free as a flag.

But enough about cars for now. We'll talk more later on about why this Lincoln is an important part of my life. Right up front, what you need to know is that I'm basically a shy person. I'd rather keep to myself, and I don't feel comfortable talking to others.

If you just met me today and saw where I live and work, if you saw how I know everybody and speak to everybody I meet, and how I constantly run this little rumble of a laugh in the back of my throat, then you'd conclude I'm an extrovert. But I'm not. I'm introverted at my core. I need silence and solitude like I need my next breath, and I make time for the quiet moments because truth whispers and the world is loud.

Look at the pictures of me as a boy, and you can see my shyness. The reticence is written all over my face. Through the years it's taken work to overcome my shyness and to learn to reach out to people. Even today I need to remind myself daily to reach out. Some mornings I get up and don't feel like going to work, but I tell myself, *Norm, get up. Your job is to be with people. Do it!*

The advantage for any introvert is that he or she is born contemplative. This ability comes instinctively. Yet the incessant pull to reflection must be continually influenced by a willingness to connect with others, or else depression can settle in. What helps me in this area is that every day now I meet with God both morning and evening and try to rest in His presence and listen for His voice and guidance. Yes, I listen for God's voice. I know that's hard to explain. There's something inside my heart that says, *This is the way to go. Walk in it. This is what you need to do.* And then I need to do it. I ask myself, will this decision bring good or not? And I make my decision based on what I believe God wants me to do. Then I live with that decision and its consequences for the rest of my life.

That pattern started for me years ago. When I was a young man, I made one big decision that changed the rest of my life. I made this decision in agreement with another person. And if we had chosen differently, yes, our lives—and the lives of many others—would have been vastly different. But I'm getting ahead of myself here.

You must understand, I don't see my life story as any big deal. Certainly no ambition has ever welled up within me to write down my life story. But others have seen the value of my story, or at least sections of it, and they have prompted me to write this book. They say, "Norm, your story can help someone," and that excites me. I don't care about fame or money or publicity or any of that. But this call to help someone. This great call to love someone. Well, holy smash, that's what life is all about, isn't it?

Over the next chapters, I'll tell the story of how I learned to love deeply and fearlessly and widely. This love benefits others. This love also benefits me. How do I dare begin to explain this love? I struggle with words. Maybe it's simply that I see God's presence in everybody, and if I love God then I need to love the people He created. That's my calling, just like it's yours. Our job is to love others "without stopping to inquire whether or not they are worthy." Thomas Merton penned that last line, and just last week some students scrawled the quote beautifully in chalk on the sidewalk where I work.

See, I've found out that the enemy of love is not hate. The enemy of love is fear. Hate is the fear that somebody will hurt us. We need to let go of the fear that imprisons us, and not allow the feelings of fear to hold us back. If we let go of our fears, then we can reach out and truly connect with others. If we learn to let go of our fears, then we can truly love.

ψ ψ ψ

It took me a long while to grasp this. I'm seventy-two now, and I wonder even at this age if I have fully caught what I need to. Yes, I believe love has a link with miracles. I grasped this even as a boy growing up in Long Beach. Inexplicable events and interactions of wonder and mystery occur throughout life, and if we are people of faith then we attribute these to providence.

Here's the story of the first miracle I remember. Before my soul came on the scene and my memory kicked in, my father, Anthony Supancheck, met my mother, Alice Bigelow, a nurse, when he worked at the limestone mines in Trona, California. They married in 1940 and moved to Long Beach so my father could take a job in the shipyards. In 1942 they started a family. I was their firstborn, and by the time I was five, my father faced a financial question. A Catholic, he had five young children by then (seven would eventually be born), and he needed more money to take care of so many children. The shipyards paid well enough, but his wages weren't enough to raise a large family.

My father prayed about his need and believed that God was moving him to start his own business. He quit his job at the shipyards and secured loans and bought land and built a building. He acquired machinery and equipment and supplies and hired workers and started his own sheet metal business. His shop was located in Signal Hill, a suburb of Los Angeles, about a mile from our home.

I can still picture his shop today. The initial building had a Spanish-style front with a high roof and sloping sides. Inside was a big room that contained all the equipment. On the right side was an office with a desk, a place for big plans. Way in the back was a storage building that housed metal and gutters and siding. My father bought copper and galvanized sheet metal and black iron. He bought a hoist for building cyclones. He had a large welding machine and a spot welder, a shear for cutting metal, and a brake for bending metal. Numerous benches were scattered about the room for cutting material and laying it out. As a five-year-old, I remember looking around the shop for the first time and simply saying, "Wow." This was where my dad worked. My dad! He was in charge of this shop, and I was proud of him. Opening his own business was a family dream come true.

When you start a business, it seldom starts with a bang. The doors opened and business was slow. Dreadfully slow. It wasn't long before my father ran out of money. One by one he let go the workers he'd hired. We cut back as a family, scrimped, and went without, but soon our cupboards were bare, our fridge empty. My father prayed for guidance and help. God had told him to start his own business, hadn't he? I don't know if this is an actual memory of something I saw firsthand or only of what I imagined, but I have this image of my father on his knees murmuring, "I don't have money to buy bread or milk for my children. God, you inspired me to start this business. And nothing's happened. I've worked as hard as I can. Now I'm at a standstill. We don't know what to do, but our eyes are on you."

No answer came. God was silent. My father had no other choice but to close his business.

It was evening, and he was literally locking the front door of his shop for the final time when a stranger came walking along the sidewalk. The stranger stopped, but it wasn't to chat. He was in a hurry, and he described a project he needed done immediately. My father started to tell him he couldn't do the job because he had no money for materials. But before my father could say anything, the man presented him with upfront money—five hundred dollars!

"To get you started," the stranger said.

Dad stared at that money. At the outstretched hand. A few seconds ticked by, seconds that seemed like forever. Then he took the money and shook the man's hand and agreed to do the job. The money was enough for Dad to buy the materials he needed for the project as well as some food for our family. The business was saved, other jobs soon came in, and from that point onward, Tony Supancheck's business—the Signal Hill Sheet Metal Shop—grew and thrived.

The stranger seemed like any flesh and blood human, yet my father always believed that God had sent him an angel. I had no reason to doubt my father. From that experience I first glimpsed how God moves in mysterious ways, ways that look different from what we first imagine. The image of a hand, not the stranger's hand, but of God's hand—outstretched to us—was seared into my mind and soul, and I have never forgotten it.

🍃 🍃 🍃

From this early age I took to heart my new, fundamental understanding of the supernatural, of how the personhood of the divine can move in our lives. But to get from a miracle to this greater call to love, this call to love others— this was something that took far longer for me to realize. I began the process by thinking straightforwardly (I guess like all little boys do), that if you love someone then you need to demonstrate your love somehow. My mother kissed us kids to show her love. Surely that was the way.

For me, her name was Charlene, and she lived in the neighborhood next to ours. We met when we were both six. We were in the same classroom at school, and she was the only girl on her block, so she often played with us. None of us kids had any money for fancy toys, so we played kickball, hide and seek, and baseball on the street. Sometimes other kids from Charlene's street picked on her, as kids are prone to do, because she was the only girl in the group. So I tried to protect her as best as a small boy could.

A vacant lot lay down the street. I enlisted the help of my younger brothers, Jim and John. Twins, they were ten months younger than I was, and we built a fort in the lot with scrap lumber. This fort was fancy. We dug down five feet and hefted plywood on top so we could hide out below and have a roof over our heads and tunnels. The grass— you could pull it up in clumps and use it for dirt clod wars against our "enemies." Sure enough, one day I was playing near the fort with Charlene, and some boys came by and threw dirt clods at her. This girl I cared about was some distance away from me when the dirt started flying, outside the protection of our fort, so I ran toward her, timid even though I was, and in defiance chucked the dirt clods back at the perpetrators. Luckily the boys stopped and ran away. Charlene was close to tears. Maybe she was already crying. Yet she wiped the dirt from the front of her blouse, looked straight at me, and, by way of saying thanks for my valiant conduct, I guessed, managed a smile.

Charlene had brunette hair and a fair complexion, almost snowy. We stayed friends for several more years. By sixth grade we were still in the same class together at school, and she was athletic by then, popular, smart, and a person of strong character who everybody respected.

By contrast, I didn't think I was that smart. I didn't get good grades. My dad believed we needed to do chores around the house rather than spend time studying. Charlene's parents encouraged her to study hard, and study often. I sat in class one day staring at the back of Charlene's hair and wondered what she was going to be like when she was older. I was noticing girls more by then. Their hair, their skin, their shapes—so different from myself.

It was rudimentary thinking about love, surely. In sixth grade, this is the sum of what churned inside my brain—I thought, *Maybe I'll marry Charlene one day. She's pretty, and that's good, because I don't want to marry a girl who'll turn out to be ugly.* I carefully studied the looks of her parents to see what Charlene might look like when she got older. Other classmates' parents didn't age well at all. They looked like old gorillas. But Charlene's parents seemed nicely preserved, so I decided to make my move.

The next afternoon I walked up to Charlene during lunch hour. I knew exactly what needed to be done. If I was going to marry this girl, then my next move was to let her know that I liked her. My heart pounded in my chest, and with each step as I walked closer to her, my hands grew clammier, my throat drier. When she was only a step away, I moved forward. Like Cupid's arrow racing toward its target, I flew toward the bull's-eye of her cheek. The flesh of my lips touched the flesh of her face, and before I could explain myself, she pulled away and slapped me hard.

The experience left me stunned and confused. I genuinely liked her, but I was shy, remember, and I had no idea how to articulate my feelings to her. I figured a kiss was all a boy needed to do when he loved a girl. Right?

When I came home I told my mother what happened. Mother had dark hair and was tall, a very handsome woman. She was kind and calm; nothing would ever upset her. But she could be firm too. "Norm, you only kiss girls when you're really interested in them," she said. "Understand?"

I nodded.

How could I tell her I was already in love with Charlene? I'd carefully extrapolated what Charlene was going to look like when she grew older, and she'd passed the test. What else was needed besides beauty and a kiss? It dawned on me then how tremendously difficult it is to find a language for love. To describe strong feelings accurately. To lay out plans for you and another person for the rest of your life.

Nothing more was ever spoken between Charlene and me. Long gone were our games in forts, our dirt clod wars, our hide and seek. From then on, I was embarrassed to be in her presence and tried to avoid her whenever possible. Decades later, we met at a school reunion. She had grown even more beautiful, I thought, even with wisps of gray in her hair and lines of living in her face. We talked easily then and laughed together effortlessly. I brought up the subject of the stolen kiss, and she said, "You know, Norm, I really liked you too. You took me by surprise, and I didn't know what to do, so I slapped you."

No, I wasn't exactly heartbroken when Charlene had slapped me. But I definitely felt rebuffed. I vowed not to try that again anytime soon. But I had hope too. Even in sixth grade, I believed God was in control of everything. I wanted to get married someday. I wanted to have kids of my own. If God wanted me to get married, then I was confident He'd guide me to the right person. I remember sort of shrugging off the whole experience and saying to myself, *Well, I guess Charlene's not the one for me.*

🍁 🍁 🍁

Let me offer one last description of love as I sketch on this canvas of introduction. Hold these images in flux, just like I'm presenting them to you now—this swirled palette of love and God and the marvelously unexpected directions He can lead a person through in life. Because that's what I hope to paint a more complete picture of in the pages ahead.

Love is like this toe I have, of all strange comparisons. Years ago, I was in a bad accident. When I awoke in the hospital after being sewn together, I discovered that the little toe on my left foot had been dislocated and not set back into place. The doctor explained, "Well, Norm, you had so much else wrong with you that we didn't bother with the toe."

Because of that toe, I walk with a limp today. A callus has formed underneath the toe, and it hits the bone, and the bone hits a nerve. How many steps does a person take in a day? Five thousand? Ten thousand? Every step I take today is painful. If I did what felt natural to me, then I'd lash out at other people because of that pain. Or I'd hide in my office and never venture out. I certainly wouldn't smile at people.

But I must walk. I walk as part of my job, because I need to visit many people. I walk at my cabin because other people use it too, so there's always work to be done—a gutter fixed, a shingle to be replaced. I even dance on occasion, because if you're alive, then you've gotta dance.

Just this morning as part of my job, I attended a funeral. I needed to walk up a hill and then walk down another hill, and each step was painful. I didn't want people to see the pain or focus on that, so I just walked as best I could and continued on. People saw the limping, I'm sure. I can't hide that. But hopefully all they remember is the love of the words that were said, or of the presence of the people in attendance, because that's what love can look like —a sore, sometimes very painful, and tender walk that's undertaken anyway.

What I'm going to paint for you now is a portrait of romance. I guess you could call it that. Perhaps it's not the kind of romantic story people are used to nowadays. No one-night stands. No bodices ripped. It's a romance of great love, of a love without boundaries, the kind of love God calls people to, and this love is not always easy to partake of nor straightforward in its approach.

As I've learned, love can bring with it an unspeakable joy. It can bring the security of a large family's support, and the significance of purposeful work accomplished.

Love can also bring with it great pain. It can be a reminder of what is no more. It can ache with each step we take.

And yet we walk on.

CHAPTER 1

Her Favorite Car

February 1967

THE MORNING SHONE BRIGHTER than a field of wildflowers, and when we walked into the hotel near the the LAX Airport, I had no idea I was about to meet a young woman who'd change my life forever.

We were definitely not at the conference to meet girls. Not young men like us. Peter was with me, and Gabe, and Danny. The four of us were all nearly out of graduate school, all serious about our studies, all intent upon the future. No, we were not daters by nature. Not us.

In the lobby, we blended with the crowd of learners heading toward the registration table. All around us people buzzed with conversation. They picked up books and folders and slapped name tags on their lapels, always talking, talking, talking. We queued up in the registration line, and Peter and Gabe and Danny conversed among themselves. They were looking over the program to determine the best seminars to attend later in the day after the keynote speech, but I stayed quiet, absorbing the atmosphere and trying to find a quiet place to land my thoughts.

We found our packets and headed off to the auditorium to hear the keynote speaker, first on the morning's agenda. I sat well insulated in the middle of a row near the front. Peter and Gabe were on my right, Danny was on my left. When two thousand people come to a conference, you want to be as close to the front of the auditorium as possible. The speaker began, and the four of us all scribbled notes furiously. The speaker gesticulated and waved his arms and reminded us of the necessity of quality education, of the noble purpose of training young people so their minds wouldn't be full of mush.

Then the speech was over, and we clapped and nodded in agreement, eager to stretch our legs before the next session began.

All around us at this conference were teachers and educators and administrators. Some taught through the school systems, some through the Catholic Church. This was a religious education conference with a lot of choices for breakout sessions. After the keynote, Peter and Gabe hightailed it off in one direction, while Danny nudged me toward a different room. The seminar he wanted to attend was called "Fishers," about interacting with people right where they live, and Danny had heard it was good.

As soon as we got to the assigned room, the seminar leader divided us up into groups and herded us toward round tables. Danny was sent to a different table, and I found myself alone in a cluster of strange faces. I wondered who I would talk to. Next to me sat an elderly woman. She looked matronly, not too threatening. My fingers tingled and I rubbed the back of my neck. The elderly woman had been teaching through her church for nearly fifty years now, she said, and patted me maternally on the knee.

A flurry of paper was passed around the room, and the seminar leader directed our attention to a particular page about using the power of story when talking about our spiritual journeys. We were instructed to divide into groups of two and tell each other the story of our relationship with God. Each person was to speak. I glanced around for Danny, but the elderly woman's gnarled hands gripped my hand strongly. As she took my hand in both of hers, she half closed her eyes and began with how her parents came to America from the *old country*, how she beat diphtheria as a child, and continued her narrative on through the years.

Secretly, I was happy she was doing all the talking. If she talked, then I didn't need to, and I was fine with that. The more she talked, the more I listened. Her story was quite intriguing actually, and I nodded occasionally and offered a low hum of affirmation whenever she caught her breath. We were nearly up to the 1930s when the seminar leader called out a cheery, "Okay—time's up. I hope each person got a chance to share." Inwardly, I grinned. I had escaped being drawn out. We turned our chairs back to face the table again, and the seminar leader directed the attention to each table leader. It was time to process the stories within each table group.

I hadn't noticed our table leader when we first sat down. There'd been too much commotion in the room. She introduced herself by her first name only—Shayla—and spoke with a warm, direct voice, guiding the discussion around our table exactly where it needed to go. She struck me instantly as a strong professional and highly capable of doing her job, even though she was as young as I was. My first thoughts about her were that undeveloped. Nothing powerful. Nothing more.

Before I knew it, the session was over. It was time for lunch, and my stomach was growling. I said good-bye to the elderly lady and searched around the room to find Danny. My face was pointed toward the far corner of the room when I heard a voice near my left shoulder.

"Boy, you sure are a good listener."

I turned. Shayla stood next to me, her hand outstretched. I mumbled a quick hello and shook her hand.

"What's your name anyway?" she asked.

"Norm," I said. "Uh, Norm Supancheck. I'm just looking for my friend Danny. We came to the conference together and it's . . ."

"I'm Shayla," she said. "Shayla Strohmeyer—and I'd like to get to know you more."

These last words of hers were that exact, and I caught myself repeating them in my mind as if I hadn't heard her correctly. She wanted to get to know me more? I didn't know how to respond to that level of bluntness. Why would she want to get to know me more? Her tone was so direct, it actually struck me as a bit brash. Any of the young women I interacted with were never this much to the point. I studied Shayla's face trying to discern what angle she was coming from. She smiled, and the ice melted. She had no gimmick, I could see that quickly. There was an undeniable genuineness in her tone. A sweetness. She went on to explain that she'd been watching me when the elderly lady shared her story with me. She'd noticed how the woman had commandeered the whole time, and how I'd just sat there listening. It was the listening that caught Shayla's attention. Listening was a rare quality in today's world, she added. Something to be highly valued.

A jacket sleeve brushed up against mine. "Hey there, I'm Danny, what's your name?" Danny had found us. Shayla's gaze broke and she turned in his direction. Before she could answer, Peter and Gabe walked into the room and up to us, fresh from another session. I carefully introduced them all to the young table leader.

Shayla jumped right in. She asked my three friends how they liked the conference so far, then immediately followed up with other questions, deeper questions. While Peter, Gabe, and Danny did the talking, I studied Shayla more closely. Her questions forced a person to express who he was and where his life was going. She was a middle school teacher, she told us, which explained how she had a way of getting a person to open up. That age group could be squirrelly, I knew, and it took a special dynamic to work with students in junior high. She was about twenty-five, same as us, slimly built, yet sturdy, with a fresh soap-scrubbed complexion and dark hair cut to her shoulders. Her eyes were blue and piercing, and her eyebrows arched mischievously whenever she smiled. She struck me as beautiful, the type of beauty where she'd blend in well on a windswept beach, or on a trail hiking through the woods on a glorious fall afternoon.

I didn't think I rated as handsome. In high school, a classmate had once quipped, "Hey Norm, you've got a big nose and little ears." When he said that, I wanted to crawl under a table and hide. I found out after I graduated that a lot of girls had actually liked me. I was built like a football player, with thick shoulders and a sort of craggy face, and I had a unique way of putting people at ease, someone told me later. But I had no idea that any girls were actually attracted to me.

Our conversation near the roundtable was almost finished. The room was empty. Lunch was calling. With the hordes of people attending the conference, it was doubtful we'd run into Shayla again. Peter, Gabe, Danny, and I said our good-byes and headed toward the door. We were three paces down the hallway when Danny swung around suddenly and said, "Just a second, guys," and broke away from us. We stood still and checked our schedules. All around us, people milled about. Danny was back in two minutes, a triumphant gleam in his eye.

"Where'd you go?" I asked.

"Made a date." Danny cupped a hand to his mouth and checked his breath.

"You did what?" Gabe said, his voice incredulous.

"I asked Shayla out," Danny said. "To my parents' house for lunch. They'll be home; don't worry." He slapped me on the back, and I clued in to what he was talking about. Danny's parents lived only two blocks from the hotel. It would sound nonchalant of him to say to Shayla something casual like, "Hey, I'm heading right around the block to my folks' house to eat. Why don't you come with me for lunch?"

"So . . . are we invited too?" Gabe asked. "I'm starving."

Just then, Shayla appeared in the doorframe. She had her book bag packed and under her arm, and she'd put on a light sweater. It clung to her in all the right ways, none of which were matronly.

Danny flashed us all a big grin. "Nope," he said.

❧ ❧ ❧

Later that evening, Danny stuck his head inside my dorm room and uttered a small groan. I was sitting at my desk, my nose buried in a textbook.

"I'm smitten," he muttered.

"You're what?" I didn't look up.

"Smitten, Norm. Seriously. You'll never guess what happened at lunch."

I glanced at the pile of homework I still needed to do that evening, turned in his direction, and set down my book. "Okay," I said. "I give up."

"So, she came over for lunch," Danny said. "But—get this—my folks weren't home after all. I don't know where they were, and I was just as surprised as she was."

"She make a run for it?"

"Nah," Danny said. "She stayed cool the whole time. Right away I offered to cook for her. She said sure, so I stuck my head into the fridge, pulled out whatever I could find, and cooked. And then—"

"What'd you eat?"

"Steaks, Norm. We ate steaks. You think I'm going to give hamburger to a girl like this? But it doesn't matter now. This is the good part—we ate, and when the meal was over she thanked me. Guess how she thanked me, Norm. Guess."

"How?"

"She kissed me."

"She kissed you? On the lips?"

"Well, no, on the cheek," Danny added quickly. "I'm sure it was nothing more than a friendly peck good-bye. But you gotta help me now, Norm. This is serious."

"Danny," I sighed. "Why are you even talking like this? We don't date girls in the profession we're heading toward."

"This is different, Norm. I just want to see her again. As soon as possible. You gotta help me. Just one date with her, that's all I ask. Look—it doesn't even need to be a date, okay. I just want to see her again. That's all."

I shifted in my chair. A girl who had that kind of power over a young man was either a girl who had something amazing to offer or a girl to be wary of. When it came to Shayla Strohmeyer, I didn't know yet which it was. Danny was so intent in his quest, so earnest in his plea, I didn't have the heart to say no to him. I gathered he wasn't wavering in his commitment to his life's calling. He wasn't actually asking to date her. He just wanted to be in her presence again. Like one would go to see a good movie twice. He'd close down the relationship before things became too serious.

"All right," I said. "What story do you have in mind to get us out of here?"

Danny grinned. "Barbecue."

"Nah, that'll never work."

"Yes it will. That's not a lie. Just lay it out for him. You'll find the right words."

I knew what Danny was getting at. We needed permission to leave the school on weekends, so we needed to think up a good reason for the principal, the rector, to let us go.

The barbecue was this: My father still operated the sheet metal shop, and, having picked up some of those skills from the time I spent working in Dad's shop, I'd offered to build a huge barbecue for the college. The barbecue would feed a hundred people at a time, and I was building it on the back of a trailer to make it mobile. What Danny was getting at was for me to ask the principal if I could go work on the barbecue over at my parents' house. I'd need Danny to help me, of course, so he could justifiably leave campus too. It wouldn't be a lie. Truly, we did need to work on the barbecue some more. I thought through the plan. It just might work. Danny shot me a grin.

Ah, the lengths friends go to for friends. The next day I went to the principal and told him I needed to go home for the weekend. I said my dad wanted me to get the barbecue out of his shop because it was taking up space. That wasn't a lie. The principal asked a few more questions, then said I could go, so I pressed the point and asked if Danny could come to help too. He asked why, and I said, "Because Danny is handy. He helps a lot." The principal kind of rolled his eyes and said, "Oh, all right."

Back in my dorm room I relayed to Danny the good news.

"One more small request, Norm," he said.

"What's that?"

"Call Shayla for me."

"What!"

"C'mon, Norm. I'll seem too desperate if I call her myself. This way, if you call, it'll make things more casual. We're just hanging out with friends then. Please!"

I tried putting this back on Danny. I tried hard. But Danny insisted. He was the one who was sweet on her, not me, but he begged and handed me her telephone number. I wasn't used to calling girls who weren't family members, but I dialed the number anyway, expecting to get Shayla's parents, or maybe a roommate. Or maybe she wouldn't be home, and Danny and I could forget the whole blessed thing.

"Hi, this is Shayla," came the cheery voice on the other end.

"Uh, hi," I said. No buffer at all. Rats. "This is Norm Supancheck. We met at the conference a few days ago, and I was just wondering . . . uh, what I mean to say is . . . Danny would like to come up and visit with you. Are you free to go to dinner this coming Saturday?"

Danny punched me in the shoulder and hissed, "Say *both* of us! Both!"

I grinned, and before I could say anything more, Shayla answered, "Sure, I'd be glad to see both of you guys."

Those were her exact words. *Both of you guys.* Shayla and I made a bit more small talk about when to meet and where. She lived with her older sister and her sister's husband, she explained. Could we meet her there? I said sure. After I hung up, Danny asked me to tell him everything Shayla said in as much detail as I could remember. I did. I offered it without commentary. One thing I kept to myself, though.

Shayla's first line made it sound as if she wanted to see me too. Not just Danny. I didn't mention that to Danny, of course. Undoubtedly I was only reading into things.

If I thought about the line one way, it made me nervous. Yet—and this other direction I had no categories for—if I thought about the line another way, it made me smile.

$$\psi \quad \psi \quad \psi$$

The following Saturday, Danny and I left the college in two cars, each of us headed in a different direction. Los Angeles is a maze of smaller cities all built together to form one gigantic, four thousand-square-mile metropolis. It can take time to drive anywhere of substance in Los Angeles, and just because you and another person both live in L.A., it doesn't mean you necessarily live near the other person.

Danny drove to his parents' home in Fullerton, in the southern part of the metro area, and I drove to my parents' house in Long Beach, which is sort of mid-center of the city, near the ocean. The college was in Camarillo, in Ventura County northwest of Los Angeles. Our plan was to take care of some odds and ends first, then meet again at my house so we could head up together that evening to Shayla's sister's house in San Pedro, west of where I lived and also near the ocean.

At first, all went according to plan. I did my laundry at home and worked a bit on the barbecue and trailer to justify my excuse for leaving school. But just before Danny was scheduled to meet me, the phone rang. It was Danny with bad news. His car wouldn't start. At that very moment he was digging into the engine, and he promised it wouldn't take long to fix.

"I'll wait here for you," I said. "I'm sure she'll understand."

"Are you kidding?" Danny said. "You don't reschedule with a girl like her. You need to keep her company for me, Norm. I'll be along soon. Please go, right now."

What could I do? I hopped in my car and headed over to San Pedro. I found the right address okay. Shayla met me at the door like she was in a hurry to get somewhere. She was outfitted in a sleeveless, flowered dress and looked ready for a night out. I quickly snapped my attention to her face. Concern clouded her eyes.

"Norm, I'm so sorry," she said, without inquiring about Danny's whereabouts. "I completely forgot I need to chaperone a dance at the junior high tonight. I'd love to go to dinner with you guys, but I can't get out of this. Why don't you just come to the dance with me? We can both be chaperones."

I was speechless. Shayla already had her clutch purse in one hand, her car keys in the other. The decision was already made, and I was going, like it or not. She tossed me her keys. "C'mon," she added. "We can take my car." I noticed a force of power accompanied Shayla's words whenever she spoke. It was difficult to know how to begin to say no to her request, much less tell her I didn't feel comfortable being alone in a car with a woman. These things were frowned upon at the college. But there we were. My car was a 1955 Chevy, an old wreck of a beast. Hers was brand new. A white 1967 two-door Pontiac LeMans. Jaunty. Sleek. Big, growling grill. Her sister Marge's husband owned a shipping company, Shayla explained offhandedly as we climbed into her car. I gathered that money wasn't much of a problem in the family.

We headed north to the dance. Right away Shayla talked and asked questions, and I found I could answer her without any hesitation. That struck me as odd, because if it had been anyone else, I would have kept quiet. We talked and talked and drove to the dance just as the sun was setting. I soon forgot about Danny. We arrived at the school and parked.

Students waved and smiled as Shayla walked into the gym. They smiled easily around her, like she was one of their favorite teachers. Everyone seemed at ease in her presence. The gymnasium was festooned with crêpe paper, balloons, and streamers. Music bopped from a record player near the stage. A punch bowl was set up along with a refreshments table piled high with home-baked cookies. Junior high students stood in gaggles of three and four. All the boys were clumped together on one side of the gym, all the girls on the other. Shayla called out to a few students by name and urged a couple more to make the first move. Slowly, the girls and boys obeyed, mixed, and began to dance with each other.

Shayla walked back toward where I'd planted myself near the refreshments table. "I'd like a glass of punch," she said. "You?" I poured a glass for her and one for me, and we picked up exactly where we'd left off. We talked about everything and nothing and then circled back to talk about everything again. The record player spun, and song after song came and went. Students danced, and we supervised, and we talked about our plans for life, what was important to us, our families, our relationships with God. I was amazed at how easily I was able to relate to her, at how openly I could express who I was. Already, I'd developed a true respect for this young woman. I'd only known her for little more than an hour, and she was already becoming one of the most captivating persons I'd ever met.

After a while, Shayla offered to show me her classroom, so I found myself walking through the empty halls of the junior high school along with her, looking at artwork on the bulletin boards and talking about the things we used to do in school when we were kids. Her classroom, even in the dark, was a blaze of color. Posters hung from the walls. All the supplies were neatly squared away in cubicles along one side. Her classroom radiated openness and order, direction and encouragement.

We'd been at the dance more than an hour when I suddenly remembered Danny.

"Hey, we've gotta get back," I said.

Shayla's eyes flashed like she understood what I was getting at. The other chaperones could handle the rest of the dance. We walked back to the gym, this time at a brisker pace, checked in with the teacher in charge, said goodbye to a few students, and then made our exit. Shayla handed me the keys again, insisting I take the wheel. Her car felt smooth compared to the jalopy I'd been driving, and as I switched on the headlights and headed out of the parking lot, I noticed Shayla gave a contented sigh and patted the inside of the car door.

"I just love riding in a bigger car," she said. "Makes you feel secure, you know? For as long as I live I never want to drive anything except a big, safe car."

I chuckled. "If you could drive any kind of a car, what would it be?"

Shayla didn't answer the question at first. It was the only lull in the conversation we'd had all evening, and she was strangely quiet for about two minutes. When she did answer, she changed subjects.

"You know I was in a convent once," she said.

"You wanted to be a nun?"

Shayla's voice sounded far away, and she stared far off into the moonlit darkness. "Two of my sisters became nuns. I've always been close to my sisters, so I thought I'd give a try to life in a convent for a while, but I didn't make it my life's work."

"How come?"

"Devotion to God wasn't the problem. Loving others wasn't an issue. It was . . ." Shayla paused, searching for words. "I don't know. I guess I've always seen myself as a strong person, and to have someone telling me what to do and when to do it didn't go over very well. The convent just wasn't for me."

I was silent now, thinking about my own commitments.

"Say Norm, Danny can wait a little while longer." Shayla's voice sprung back to its usual brightness. "Let's take Palos Verdes Drive home. It's so pretty along the cliffs by the ocean. It's my favorite road in all Los Angeles. Let's do it, okay?"

The route down Palos Verdes Drive West was longer, that was true, but Danny was my friend. I couldn't quite shake the feeling I was honing in on his special evening, on a friendship with a girl that he had followed up on, not me. Still, I wasn't about to say no to Shayla. Not at this stretch of the conversation. I eased her car onto the drive.

"You never told me what your dream car is," I said.

Shayla looked over at me and I glanced in her direction. Her blue eyes caught the gleam of oncoming headlights and she looked into my eyes for a moment before I set them back on the road. I thought I saw a sliver of sadness in her eyes, but this time she answered quickly, and with a grin.

"Why, a Lincoln, of course."

CHAPTER 2

A Question Rises in Me

I WAS QUITE NERVOUS driving along the cliffs of Palos Verdes, not because of the cliffs, but because of the tension between my friendship with Danny and my new liking of Shayla. I wanted to get back quickly for Danny. But around Shayla, my shyness dissipated like morning fog. In her presence I felt something I'd never felt before. This new and pleasant feeling was being generated still, and I had no words for it yet. It was being created in my soul as if out of nothing. The moon hung low over the Pacific Ocean, and at places during our drive down the scenic highway, I stole glances westward out Shayla's window and glimpsed the horizon stretched out eternally against the darkened evening sky.

"Stop the car here." Shayla's voice bore the slightest lilt.

"What? Where? We're in the middle of nowhere."

"Over there!"

The car slowed and gravel crunched under the tires. We stopped. I turned off the ignition and set the parking brake. Shayla said, "I want to show you my favorite spot."

I walked with her toward the edge of the cliff. She grabbed my hand in hers and added, "It's absolutely beautiful and this is the perfect night with the moon shining on the sea." My first instinct was to let go of her hand, but I didn't. Shayla's hand felt warm and small inside mine, and in my mind I mulled the presence of her fingers. Slender. Feminine. So different from mine. I have hands the size of canned hams. Huge fingers useful for pounding sheet metal. For holding a football. A lump slid down my throat. Shayla and I kept walking toward the edge of the cliff, our hands still joined.

She led me to a rock overlooking the ocean. There, she let go of my hand. The rock was perfect for sitting down and so we sat down together. There was not a lot of room, so we sat very close.

All was quiet except for the pounding of the surf below us. The moon was bright and shining, and it left a trail of light on the ocean in front of us that glimmered and danced on the water. The air was cool with the night breeze. Shayla put her arm around my shoulders. My heart started to dance like the light on the water.

"What do you see, Norm?" Her voice was soft.

What did I see? In front of me I saw only beauty. Waves and breakers crashing on the rocks below us. An expansive sky with multicolored hues of evening darkness. Moonlight. A seagull flying by intent on some unknown destination. I closed my eyes, trying to take a mental picture of this moment. Images blurred, and in my mind's eye, I saw my dorm room back at the seminary. It was a simple room with a single bed, a dresser, and a basic desk with a hard-backed wooden chair. The room communicated the dedication that lay in the direction I was heading. A direction I was unquestionably heading toward alone. Yet here I was, sitting beside this young woman in the dark.

"We can't forget Danny," I said. But I made no effort to stand.

Shayla was quiet a moment. Then she murmured, "Right. Danny." She remained sitting too.

We sat without moving for perhaps another five minutes. Then we got up. We walked slowly back to the car and we held hands this way too. I opened the passenger-side door for her, then walked around to the other side, started her car, and put it in gear. We were on the road once more, back to see my friend Danny.

✤ ✤ ✤

Danny's car sat waiting in Shayla's sister's driveway.

He wasn't upset when Shayla and I walked inside. He was chatting amiably with Marge, and when he saw us, he simply asked how our evening had been.

"It was fine," I said. It was hard to answer because so much was going on in my head.

Shayla grinned and asked Danny how he was. He said that he had a great time talking to Marge. We talked about Danny's car a bit. The problem with the engine was fixed now and all was well. Marge went into the kitchen and brought out some sodas and snacks for us. Shayla helped. We stayed another twenty minutes or so. Not long. It was getting late and we both had to return home, go to Sunday Mass, and then, after visiting our families, return to the seminary.

Danny took his car back to the seminary. I took mine. Neither of us spoke anymore about Shayla. Danny seemed happy to see her one more time, even for twenty minutes. His thirst for her presence seemed quenched. He didn't talk about dating her ever again, and he didn't ask me to help him contact her.

But Shayla contacted me.

Those were the 1960s after all, the decade of empowered women, and she had no hesitation speaking her mind or calling up a young man to talk on the phone. Shayla struck me as a modern, confident young woman, and her contacting me wasn't for a date either, which is perhaps why neither of us was fazed. A few days later she phoned and asked me to help her with a youth retreat she was participating in as leadership staff. The program was officially called Youth Encounter, and the Catholic Church held a weekend retreat every three or four weeks for high school students. The request was legitimate. About two hundred students came to each retreat, and putting one on was no small matter. It took about forty staff to organize and run each retreat. Shayla was always on the lookout for quality staff, she added.

I said yes. It sounded like fun. I was in the business of learning to help people, after all, and it was easy to receive permission from the rector to leave campus for a church-sponsored event such as this. I went and helped out at the retreat. Then Shayla asked me to help out at a second one. I helped out at that. And then there was a third. And a fourth. And a fifth. I became a regular.

Shayla worked as a Spanish and English as a second language teacher at Ridgecrest Intermediate School in Palos Verdes and in her spare time she loved to volunteer with the Youth Encounter retreats, which weren't part of her regular school responsibilities. She'd grown up in a strong Catholic home—she was the eighth of nine children, and she loved God and people. So she enjoyed helping people any way she could, especially people who were struggling with life problems, which is common with teens.

Some of the students who came to the retreats had faith-based backgrounds and some didn't. They came from parishes around L.A. County, or they knew friends who went to the retreats, and the friends invited them along. The retreat center was at Westlake. It was located in a beautiful wooded area off the road on the way up to Ventura and Santa Barbara.

The camp was nestled beside the lake and there were boats, a large eating area, a meeting room, a playing field, and some primitive cabins for overnight stays. From Friday evening until Sunday afternoon we held general sessions where a speaker encouraged kids to get to know themselves better, to grow in their faith and maturity, and to grow in relationships with their parents, friends, and God. We had about two hours of recreation. Crafts. Games. Sports. Just hanging out. After each talk we would gather in small groups of about ten people to share our thoughts about what had been said. Before each meal we said a blessing. Some kids would bow their heads and others wouldn't. That was okay—we welcomed them all. We did exercises in trust where a circle of people would link arms and one person would fall into their arms. We took yarn, poster paper, and strips of leather and made necklaces, bracelets, name tags, hats, and flower montages. In the evenings around a campfire, someone always had a guitar. We sang "This Is the Day" and "This Little Light of Mine," and "It's a Brand New Day."

One of the consistent themes during the retreats was the need for each person to open up and talk with others. This proved a big jump for me, particularly as a staff member. Yet that's what happened. Everyone spent a lot of time just talking about life, God, family, and friendships. Even me.

Shayla was a natural leader. Many times I caught an unguarded view of her out of the corner of my eye. She'd be talking to a kid who was going through a hard time and be completely focused on that kid. The way Shayla's eyes would be set, I could tell she was completely listening, completely engrossed. These were moments when I knew she was being her genuine self. Not that she was ever guarded with me. But these moments confirmed her selflessness. These moments proved the depth of her character. When it came to serving others, Shayla was the real deal.

We had our share of tough kids come through the retreat program. Kids who'd been hurt, or who were walking through deep waters in their home lives or at school. One student's father was an alcoholic and was being abusive toward the family. Another student felt alienated from the people around her and was contemplating suicide. Another was toying with drugs and rebellion. The atmosphere of the retreats was deliberately crafted to encourage kids to open up and receive support. It was amazing to see the joy spread, the friendships made, and the kids who once were quiet now smiling and really enjoying the time with people who only a few hours ago were strangers.

Retreat after retreat proved powerful. Kids' lives were changed. And so were the lives of the staff. I'd had very little experience with retreats when I was in high school myself. I was always working at my dad's shop. But all this listening to people, all this helping them to understand things, all this focus on others—it all changed me. It opened me up. When I felt shy, I learned to realize that the focus was more on me—on how uncomfortable I felt. But when I purposefully climbed out of my shell, then that took the focus off me and put it onto other people, where it was needed.

One of my favorite times came right after each retreat was over. Shayla and I went out to eat and talk. We went to Denny's usually, a few miles away from the retreat center, and slid into a quiet booth in the corner of the restaurant, ordered hamburgers and Cokes, and talked for hours. We talked about what went right. About what we could do better next time. About what we saw happening with the kids. And then we'd talk about ourselves. We'd see things in the kids and reflect on our own lives and upbringings.

After eating, I'd take her home and give her a hug good-night. She'd hug me right back. She was becoming my best friend. My best female friend, anyway, and I'd never had such a close female friend. Never.

A couple of times in that wonderful season of life, Shayla and I found ourselves with a rare day off when we both had nothing scheduled. Once we went up to the hills surrounding L.A. We sat on a rock as the sun was setting and looked out over the twinkling lights of the entire L.A. basin. I put my arm around her and we sat there talking and enjoying the view until the evening fell. Almost on reflex, I kissed her. Without hesitation, she kissed me back. We just sat there afterward, enjoying the view. I guess first kisses can be monumental, but this kiss didn't seem that way. The kiss wasn't heavy. Just a peck on the lips. Her mouth was warm and soft. It just felt right.

Another time, we hiked into a valley filled with trees. A stream ran below us. Squirrels frisked about, and birds hopped above us on tree branches. The sun was out and the air shone warm on our faces. I kissed her some more then. This was all new to me, and she didn't seem to mind at all. I suppose we should have had a conversation where we tried to define our relationship, but Shayla and I didn't try to define things between us. It just seemed obvious that we liked each other. No labels existed. We didn't call each other boyfriend and girlfriend. We were just Shayla and Norm.

Shayla acted the part of the teacher in our friendship since I'd lived a sheltered life in many ways. I'd heard the term "French kissing" and wondered what that was. One day we were at her sister's house in Palos Verdes, talking, in the parlor by ourselves.

"Shayla," I said. "We've gotten pretty close, and I hear these terms and I don't know what they are."

"Okay," she said. "Put your mouth next to mine."

She demonstrated

I thought, *Wow —that is really something else.* But we didn't do it again after that. It seemed beyond what was necessary, and misleading of the genuine friendship that was growing between us.

We were able to talk freely about everything that can happen between a young man and woman, including sex. In our minds, sex was reserved for marriage alone, and so we didn't go any further in our physical relationship. We both wanted a virtuous relationship, one where we stayed close to God. I was at peace with that decision. She was going to marry someone someday, and if it wasn't me then I wanted to be able to look her husband squarely in the eye and let him know I had never fooled around with his wife.

Overall, my friends at the seminary—Danny, Peter, and Gabe—were oddly "for" our relationship, even though none of us ever dated. They'd seen a change in me since I started spending so much time with Shayla. I wasn't as quiet anymore. I smiled all the time. I seemed much happier. They were happy for us.

Every once in a while Danny and I went camping and fishing on the Kern River. He had a similar upbringing as me, and he'd never had a girlfriend either, although he was good looking, athletic, and smart. We set up the tent and hiked to the river and cast into the Kern with fishing poles. We caught a fine string of trout and cooked them freshly on the campfire that night. When the embers burned low, he and I got to talking.

"Norm," he said one evening. "Do you ever wonder what might happen between you and Shayla in the future?"

I poked the fire with a stick, shook my head, and said, "I try not to."

"It's not that long until our ordination. What are you going to do then?"

"I don't know." I looked intently into the flames. "I guess we'll always be friends."

"Really?"

Danny wasn't probing too deeply. He was just raising the obvious question, the question I needed to be grappling with far more than I was. I wasn't sure exactly what was happening between Shayla and me. She was my close friend, wasn't she? My best friend. Why would that friendship ever need to change? The world had suddenly opened up to me. I felt brighter, more alive, happier than I'd ever been. Shayla was showing me a world full of color and life, a world so opposite from the reserved person I was at my core. Still, I could see Danny's point, and from that perspective, it felt like Shayla and I were speeding toward a red light. One day soon, our romance would need to stop. I realized that for the first time I had called it "romance" in my mind. But I quickly added, "If that's what it is."

My parents, brothers and sisters, and cousins gathered on Thanksgiving Day that year, and I brought Shayla over to my parents' house after we attended Mass together in the morning. We ate a light snack at noon, then settled in to watch bowl games on TV. Shayla sat next to me and cheered whenever our team scored a touchdown. In the early evening we settled in for a feast—roast turkey with all the trimmings, mashed potatoes, savory dressing, and green bean casserole with those crunchy onions on top. Pumpkin pie with whipped cream for dessert. We ate and talked and laughed. Every once in a while I snuck glances in Shayla's direction. She was right in the thick of things, and she fit in well with our family.

I wasn't alone in my observation. My sister-in-law cornered me alone in the kitchen afterward.

"Norm," she said. "Did you notice how Shayla looks at you? She really loves you, you know." Her voice wasn't happy.

I tried to brush it off, saying we were just friends, but she persisted.

"You're in seminary, Norm. You're training to become a priest."

"I know that." I wasn't smiling now.

"I'm just saying you need to be careful, that's all." Her voice was firm. "For Shayla's sake, as well as yours."

"What are you trying to say?"

"I'm saying that close relationships like you have with Shayla only end one of two ways. You either break up, or you get married. There are no other options."

No other options.

Those three words stuck in my head. That night when I dropped Shayla off at her sister's house I was still thinking about them. I gave Shayla a quick kiss good-night, and those words stuck with me as I drove back to the seminary alone. My sister-in-law was right, wasn't she? I'd been on a one-track route to the priesthood ever since early high school days. What was I going to do now?

☙ ☙ ☙

It's funny, but even in my mid-twenties, I wasn't thinking a lot about the ramifications of my career yet, even though they were nearly upon me. It was just a track I was on, and I'd been on it for so many years I didn't give it much head space.

Years earlier, my eighth-grade teacher had recommended that I take the entrance test for the high school seminary at Our Lady Queen of Angels in Mission Hills, California. At the high school level, the subjects studied in seminary were similar to a public school, except that religious studies were added and we were all boys discerning if God was calling us to serve His people as priests. The implication was that some—but not all—students in the seminary track would become priests, and it was considered an honor to be included in the program. I told my teacher I wasn't smart enough or holy enough for seminary, but she said to take the exam anyway. I was surprised when I was accepted and was even more surprised when they put me in the highest-level group.

When high school was finished, I headed to college at Saint John's Seminary in Camarillo, California. It was part of the educational system I was used to by then, and it seemed a natural progression forward. My major in college was philosophy and my minor was Spanish. Saint John's was just a regular college in many ways. We played a lot of sports—basketball, baseball, soccer, handball. I was involved in photography, and sometimes in the afternoons after classes I'd go to the darkroom and develop pictures. I studied Latin, soon spoke it fluently, and became head of the Latin club.

We were all men from the high school, with the addition of some who came in from other high schools or colleges. By then I was used to being only with guys. I made good friends in college, and we often talked about theology and ministry in addition to our regular subjects. From our science course, some of us formed a rocket club and built rockets that we shot off out in the desert. One rocket was ten feet tall and six inches in diameter. A friend developed an infrared guidance system for a science project as well as an electronics system for our rocket that could tell us where it was, how hot it was, if it was spinning—all kinds of things. The students I hung around with were all sharp guys, astute and intelligent. I loved my college days.

We didn't consider ourselves different from the rest of the culture around us. We didn't even dress that differently—not when we were outside the school, anyway. In high school, when we were on campus, we wore a uniform of black pants, white shirt, tie, and an Eisenhower jacket—a light coat that zipped up at the front. We wore regular clothes outside school. College was the same way. On campus we wore a school uniform, a black robe called a cassock. Outside the school we dressed in regular shirts and pants.

High school was four years, and college another four years, and graduate school another four years after that. Following college, I pursued a master's degree in applied theology from Graduate Theological Union. All of the schools I attended were within the Archdiocese of Los Angeles school system, and graduate school (St. John's Theology) was the natural step forward after attending St. John's College. We learned more about the specific functions of the priesthood then. We studied the Bible and the history of the faith. We took classes in ethics and morality. We learned Hebrew and Greek, the original biblical languages, and studied the writings of early Church fathers such as Augustine and Jerome. We learned about practical pastoral ministry—how to counsel and teach, how to organize and lead a church, and how to conduct weddings and funerals. We also grew in our prayer life and our relationship with God.

I knew the Church had its share of struggles. We studied some of the great theological debates of past years, such as the controversies surrounding Athanasius and Arius. Some said Jesus wasn't fully divine. Some argued He wasn't truly human. It felt good to grow in understanding our faith and seeing how it became clarified over the centuries through many controversies.

We studied some of the stickier traditions of our faith. Priests in the Western Church weren't allowed to marry, but it was okay in the Eastern Church. I was in the Latin rite, the Western or Roman Catholic Church, and in my branch of the faith, the Church taught that a priest must dedicate his life completely to serving God. The issue wasn't that marriage was considered wrong. Far from it. The Church supported and encouraged strong marriages. The Bible itself notes that some of the early apostles were married. Saint Peter had a mother-in-law, so he must have been married. Saint Philip had five daughters who went with him on his missionary journeys. The Bible doesn't say much about Philip's wife, but he must have been married to have had that many children. But when it came to priests marrying, the Western Church recognized that marriage takes time, energy, and attention. A married man must devote his life to his wife and children. A priest must be free to bring God's word and grace to everybody, anytime. Day or night. Year after year.

I could see the Church's point and had grown to agree with it, although reluctantly. I saw the reasoning even more as my friendship with Shayla developed. For instance, Shayla and I didn't always get along, and that needed work and time. Once we went to a gathering of leaders to work on a retreat. I picked her up and drove her to the meeting. I was happy to see her, but when we went inside the house, immediately she started talking to everybody else. Something about this evening put me off. I felt shy without her, robbed of an evening in her presence. I spent most of the evening slinking around the food table.

"Shayla," I said on the drive home. "We came to this thing tonight together, and yet we weren't together. What's the deal?"

Her eyebrows lowered. "We've talked about this, Norm. When I'm with you, I'm one hundred percent with you. When we're with others, I'm with them. You need to understand that." The atmosphere was icy for a few minutes until I realized she was right. I could see that a marriage between any two people would take work. Even if you loved someone wholeheartedly. Even if you felt so much joy in your heart every time you were with that person. It was true—occasionally spouses don't see eye to eye. It takes time and emotional effort to work things through. To come to understandings. To never drift apart.

The closer Shayla and I became, the more pressing within me became the question of what to do with the rest of my life. Early each morning, I started the day with prayer. Late each evening, I ended the day with prayer.

What is my calling, Lord? I prayed, and this became a familiar prayer around that time. *What do you want with my life? What will bring me happiness? How can I best serve you?*

There was no question I was headed for the priesthood.

But this new query began to form in my mind. Perhaps, I wondered, had I completely misread God's calling for my life?

CHAPTER 3

The Road to Serving Others

LOVE. WHAT DID BEING IN LOVE MEAN to a young man headed toward the priesthood? I mulled over this question as I helped out at another youth retreat. From the corner of my eye I watched the beautiful young Shayla Strohmeyer every chance I got. When the retreat was over, I took her out to dinner. When she talked, I couldn't help but notice again how, when she spoke about working with young people, about helping to make a difference in the lives of the next generation, she absolutely glowed from the inside out. During a rare lull in the conversation, I studied her face some more. I looked at her deeply. I studied her eyes. Her mouth. The unmistakable way her hair framed her face.

"Norm," she said. "Did I ever tell you the real reason why I like big cars so much?"

I dumped ketchup on my plate, dipped in a French fry, and threw it down the hatch. "Big cars make you feel protected."

She paused a moment, and I noticed her hamburger sat untouched on her plate. "Yeah, but there's more to it." Her voice went quiet.

Shayla never held anything back from me. Not yet, anyway. But for some reason her words now seemed stuck in her throat. I wondered why. I decided to circle the wagons and try the indirect approach.

"I've got a question for you," I said. "You told me you were once in a convent, and you left because it wasn't right for you. Yet, you are here with me, and we're spending a lot of time together, and I'm in seminary. You don't seem to have a problem with that. How come?" It was a mouthful for me. These deep conversations were still very new to me, and I wasn't sure how she'd handle the question. But Shayla looked relieved to talk about something else, not the big car question.

"You're headed in the direction you know as best," she said simply. "Sometimes directions change. The most important thing is to find where God wants you to be and what God wants." She shrugged. There wasn't any hint of pretense or pressure in her words. No agenda. No play on words. I ate another handful of French fries.

By then I had learned a lot about Shayla's upbringing, but I knew I didn't know everything. I knew she was the second youngest of nine children. Her family had run out of names for babies by the time she came along, so they kind of made up a name for her—Shayla always kidded her family about that. Her mother and father were originally from Kansas City. Her dad had played professional baseball in his young adult days, but when the Depression hit, he was out of a job. The family had five children by that point, and Shayla's mom wanted the family to move to the country, so they packed up and moved to McAllen, Texas, to a sixty-acre spread with orchards of grapefruits and oranges. Shayla's dad got a job in a commercial laundry in addition to working with the family on the farm. He played semipro ball on the side. The family was close, and everybody got along well. There was a pretty big age gap between the older kids and the younger ones, so most of them were out of the house by the time Shayla came along. Shayla adored her parents and she was particularly close to her youngest brother, Keevin.

"Directions change, Norm," Shayla said again, and sipped her Coca-Cola through a straw. "Even the Catholic Church changes." Here she grinned and added, "I didn't set out to be a school teacher at first, you know. I wanted to be a nurse. I was living with my sister in San Pedro and going to the Catholic high school. Two of my older sisters, Sandy and Marian, were nuns, so I just figured becoming a nun was the right direction for me too. They were with the Sisters of Mercy over in Saint Louis. I went there for college and took a few nursing courses, but soon I changed directions and decided to go into teaching instead."

"What made you change your mind?" My mouth was full.

"Couldn't handle the sight of blood." Shayla looked to a far-off corner of the restaurant, and I understood this was not a joke. Then she snapped her attention back toward me and added, "Altogether, I was in the convent for seven years. The nuns trained me, and I'm grateful to them for that."

The waitress came by, and we both ordered dessert. Hers, a banana split. Mine, a chocolate sundae with extra whipped cream. When the waitress left to put in our order, Shayla started talking again. This time her brow was furrowed. "School should be all about the kids, and that wasn't the focus where I trained," she said. "That should be the only question that matters—What's good for the kids? Really, it was a series of things that caused me to leave. I noticed little compromises here and there. Inflexibility on the rules. Legalism. The clincher came one day when some kids didn't have enough money for textbooks. The nuns told me not to give these kids any textbooks. This was ridiculous, so I gave books to the kids anyway. The nuns weren't happy with me, so I left and came back to California. I knew then that being a nun wasn't for me. I just couldn't be held under by inflexible rules like that. I'm sure they're not all that way. But I didn't want to take another chance."

Shayla definitely wasn't one for rigidly sticking to the rules, but she only broke them with the best of intentions; I'd give her that much. I grinned and asked, "So . . . what's the real reason you like big cars?"

🌵 🌵 🌵

Shayla didn't answer me that evening at Denny's. Our desserts came, and she switched topics again . . . this time with questions aimed at me. What did I dream about? Where would I live if I could live anywhere in the world? How did I imagine my life would turn out when I reached the end of my days? I talked myself silly, then drove her home and kissed her good night, and on my drive back to seminary, I thought about how strange it was for Shayla and me to have a deep friendship where so much of the intimacy was based on the things that we talked about. I'd simply never witnessed a relationship where the conversations were like that.

In my previous experience with relationships, there was never much communication. My father never talked. Sure, he had a good sense of humor and he was good at joking around with folks, but he'd never have a deep conversation with anybody, at least not that I ever saw. My mother was the same way—reserved. She would have coffee and talk with her friends, but neither of my parents ever got into those reflective, who-am-I, what-should-I-do-with-my-life sorts of conversations that Shayla and I delved into so often.

The reticence for thoughtful communication, I think, stemmed from the cultural milieu in which my parents grew up. Dad was raised on a farm. His job was to work, not talk. Talking was considered a waste of time. Why talk when you could plow a field, fix a fence, or milk a cow? The emphasis on keeping his mouth shut wasn't conscious in his mind; it was just the way it was. When the Depression hit, the farm in Kimball, Nebraska, where he worked with his father went belly up. My grandfather went back to the family farm in David City. Dad had no money, so for two years he rode the trains and worked odd jobs wherever he could make a buck. When his money ran out, he had to beg for food. He saw some ugly things along the way, things I know he tried to forget. Once he saw a man robbed at knifepoint for food. Another time, he saw a man killed because of food. When he recalled them, these experiences made him shudder, but he pressed forward as best he could, always believing God would take care of him, no matter how hard things were.

Dad tried anything he could to make money. He even took up competitive boxing, though it wasn't a very organized sport back then. Smaller fights were called "smokers" in those days, and various private clubs held them from town to town. The fights were bare knuckled and often bloody. It was a rough way to make a buck, but he was tough and usually won.

My mother's father was an alcoholic, and he wasn't much of a conversationalist except with his drinking buddies. Mom's mother, my grandmother, had to support the family. They lived in Winnipeg, Canada. She worked as a milliner, a maker of women's hats, and when she wasn't at work, she was cooking, cleaning, and taking care of kids. One day, my grandmother, mentally and physically exhausted, was so fed up with my grandpa's drinking that she hauled all the furniture out of the house and burned it. When my grandfather came home, drunk as usual, she said to him, "We're moving to California. You can stay here or come with us." He chose to go with his family, sobered up, and eventually landed a job as a maintenance man on a large orange orchard in Whittier.

Mom graduated from high school, then worked as a nurse at Queen of Angels Hospital in Los Angeles. She was unwavering in her dedication to the patients. In 1933, when the big earthquake in Long Beach affected all of Southern California, she stayed stalwartly by her patients' sides, even though everybody else ran out of the building. Later, one of her patients said to her, "You were so calm," and Mom thought, "If you only knew." Her knees were shaking too, but, like my father, she had a tremendous sense of trust that God would protect her and work everything out in His way and time.

Sure, my parents loved me. They loved all of us kids, and we knew it. They just didn't talk to us deeply as part of their love. When we were little, Dad would come home after work at the shipyards and play with us. He was very strong, and he'd throw us up in the air and catch us. Or we'd run at his knees and he'd flip us over. He'd lay on the floor and have us stand on his hands. "Touch the ceiling, Norm," he'd say. And I'd reach for the heavens.

We always went to church as kids. I never remember a time when we didn't. When I was young, maybe eight years old, my brothers and I were whispering in church one Sunday morning. For some reason that day we were sitting all by ourselves, and the lady behind us tapped us sternly on the shoulders and hissed, "I know who you are, you Supancheck boys, and I'm going to tell your parents on you."

We all got really scared because of what Dad might do to us. As loving as he was, he also had a temper. One time we kids had been making a lot of noise roughhousing, and he came in and hit us all once with the belt. We all started crying and it was finished. You'd think we would have learned our lesson, but we did it again a few minutes later. Dad came in swinging with the belt then too. No major damage was done—maybe a welt on a backside or two. Dad just wanted us to shape up. That was the way he'd learned to toe the line. Fortunately, that lady behind us in church never squealed on us like she said she would.

When I was seven, I received my first Communion. We went through classes at school first, maybe thirty kids or so all together. Every day during first and second grade, we had been prepping for this moment. Along with our regular math, history, and spelling courses, we were taught that God draws near. God isn't distant. He's known in the Bible by the name "Emmanuel," a word that means "God with us." Our First Holy Communion was when we formally recognized His nearness.

On that momentous day, all of us kids dressed up—boys in white shirts, ties, and black suit pants, girls in white dresses—and we walked up to the front of the church in a line. Our parents sat behind us. The priest said, "The body of Christ," and we all said "amen," and then we received the wafer for the first time. We called it "the Host," and it tasted to me just like a cracker. Children don't receive the cup yet, because it's filled with real wine. After our First Holy Communion everybody went to the church hall and took a bunch of pictures. Then we went home and had a big family party with casseroles and cake.

My First Holy Communion proved to be a powerful moment for me. Even at that young age, I felt the presence of Someone larger than me, Someone greater than me, Someone beyond me. When I received the wafer, I actually shed a few tears. I ordinarily never cried, even at that young age, but it was such a moment of complete awe. God's presence felt heavy and weighty and solemn on my shoulders. He was with me, and inside of me, and filling me with His presence. Where He was, there was joy and life.

Faith surrounded us as kids. It was in our homes. Our communities. Our schools. The examples of faith modeled to us weren't always perfect, but by and large, the people surrounding us did their best to set good examples. I believe that to this day.

I'm left-handed, but around that time, one of my teachers insisted that I write with my right hand. For some reason, she considered it abnormal to be left-handed. I tried to please her, but my right-handed penmanship was so sloppy that she gave me a D. I got mad and defied her by switching back to writing with my left hand.

In third grade, I began serving as an altar boy with a group of friends. Our job was to help the priests with whatever needed doing. The priests all said the Mass in Latin in those days, so we responded in Latin while holding their books for them. We brought the bread and wine to the priests, washed their hands, and helped them dry. During Mass, we rang the church bells, which was always fun. But afterward, one priest always rapped our heads with his knuckles. I don't think he was doing it to be mean, because he did it with the sort of good-natured nonchalance an older man would display when tousling a boy's hair. It wasn't particularly painful either, but I didn't like it and even then the action didn't seem consistent with the tenderhearted affirmation the Lord himself demonstrated whenever he was around children.

Most of the teachers at my school were nuns and in high school my teachers were priests, but I never related terribly well to any of them. None of the priests I knew were bad guys, but I tended to view them as authority figures only, superiors but not role models. I tended to come late to class a lot in those days, so I was often getting written up for detentions. That was the extent of my shenanigans. There was one priest in our parish I liked, but he made a disparaging remark about me once at a school dance, so I didn't like him after that.

Sure, I'd goof around at school occasionally and toss an eraser at some-body or put a dead bug on someone's chair, but when it came to following a straight path, that was the only path I ever followed. I wasn't a troublesome kid. I never rebelled against my parents or faith or the law. We Supancheck boys were always working at Dad's shop, so there really wasn't enough time for us to get into trouble. After school. Saturdays. Holidays. During summer vacation. We were always working. Working, working, working.

While all that work might have kept me out of trouble, the only time we ever shaded into gray territory, strangely enough, was when it came to working. This was Dad's doing, and I didn't have my own opinions about the matter to the extent that I'd ever question Dad's leadership. On random days the union rep would drive up in his little green Ford. As soon as we saw that car, we knew we had to skedaddle out of the shop and jump the fence as quickly as our feet would move us. Dad's shop may have been small and family-owned, but that didn't matter to the union—their job was to see to it that only union men worked there. If the man saw us boys working, then he'd yank all the union men out of the shop as retribution, and that would sink Dad. We boys were too young to be unionized. You needed to be eigh-teen and go through an apprenticeship program first. Years later, I did end up joining the union. But as kids, it was all about working for Dad first, asking questions later.

In eighth grade came confirmation. We kids had been in religion classes for eight years by then. For the ceremony, we all wore red robes. The color symbolized the presence of the Holy Spirit, and it was meant to remind us how the Holy Spirit brings life to people. The bishop anointed us with oil on our foreheads and then we all took Communion. Again, the moment proved to be powerful for me. I felt filled with the presence of God.

I took my faith seriously and sincerely, even as a young teen. I spent time praying, reading Scriptures, and listening for God's voice. I sensed early on that God is good and that He loves us and He wants to work with us. That's how my calling began to form. It was no lightning bolt. No writing in the sky. Just a straight track toward serving others. I was Catholic. I loved God. Why wouldn't I become a priest? The only thing holding me back was that I really didn't see myself as intelligent or pious enough for the priesthood. I had yet to learn the important fact that God always uses ordinary people as His instruments of service. The Apostle Paul began life as a hardened legalist who persecuted the Church. Peter started out as an unschooled fisherman, headstrong and defiant. Thomas doubted Jesus. James and John bickered over who would be the most important when they got to heaven. I needed to see that if God used them, flawed as they all were, then God could use anyone—even me. But that realization would only come with time.

The high school seminary, Our Lady Queen of Angels, was about forty miles north of our family's house, so as a teenager I lived in a dorm during the week and came home on weekends. My parents took me and several of my classmates to the trolley from Long Beach to downtown Los Angeles; then we boarded a bus to San Fernando and took a cab to the seminary from there. Sometimes one of the parents in the neighborhood drove. It took about an hour either way.

Only one in ten students who went through the seminary track of Catholic school education ended up becoming a priest. I thought it would be a miracle if I made it through, but my teachers never pressured me or anyone in that direction that I ever saw. They gave us input, deepened our knowledge about Scriptures, taught us the history of God's working with people, and let us make up our own minds from there. Alongside all the regular school subjects, we learned the biblical languages of Latin, Hebrew, and Greek. And we played sports—Football, baseball, racquetball, soccer, basketball. You name it, we played it. The schools I went to aimed to build us up spiritually, physically, mentally, and scholastically.

Maybe just not emotionally. At least, that's how it went for me.

I was so shy in high school that I seldom participated in class discussions. At the start of my senior year one of my professors took me aside and said, "Norm, you'll never make a good priest. A good priest talks to people. If you're going to be a priest, then you're going to need to be out there relating to people. I look at you right now, and you don't have a lot of friends, you don't answer any questions in class, and you have a hard time talking to people at the dinner table. You listen a lot, but you don't talk. I don't think you should be a priest."

That criticism hit me hard. I knew I needed to do something about it, so I basically willed myself to become more of an extrovert. I started deliberately raising my hand more often to contribute in class. I knew a lot of the guys, but none of us were very close, so I started saying hello to them more, trying to deepen our friendships. I joined clubs and became the photographer for the yearbook.

The way forward wasn't easy for me. I started using Dad's high-quality twin-lens reflex camera, and I even learned how to process and develop black and white photographs. Word got around quickly, and pretty soon people started asking me to take pictures of school plays and parties and for their passports and even weddings. Though they promised to help out with the costs of the photography supplies, no one ever did, even when I gave them bills. I didn't have much money, certainly not enough to buy pictures for all these people. What was wrong with me? The question weighed on me heavily.

That priest was right—I couldn't work with people. I had no business trying to become a priest. I was a doormat, a pushover, a failure. I felt so down in the dumps that Peter, Gabe, and Danny noticed, those same three friends who were with me later when I met Shayla. They decided to hold an intervention to help me out. Late one afternoon they took me to an old shed on campus where sports equipment was kept. They told me I looked depressed and that they wanted to get to the bottom of it.

"Nah, no one really cares about me," I said.

"Yes they do," Danny said. "We all do. We're here now, and we're not going anywhere until you believe that."

They kept pressing me, saying that they cared about me, that I was important to somebody—to them in particular. But I refused to believe it. I brought up everything I'd ever felt miserable about. I didn't think I was smart. I didn't think I was good-looking. I didn't think I had any gifts worth sharing with others. I certainly wasn't quality enough material to become a priest.

We talked all night until the next morning. They kept pressing me and pressing me, and I kept resisting them and resisting them. There was no light in the shed except the candles they kept lighting. Finally at about 6:00 a.m., I broke. Something changed inside me, and I believed them. They'd stuck with me. They hadn't left. They cared about me— at least enough to stay up all night with me in the hopes of convincing me that I had value. That was enough for now.

Through their example, I saw firsthand the power of caring for others— in this case, of caring for myself. Because people had shown me love, I began to realize how important love was—not just for me, but for everybody. Maybe this calling of the priesthood would be something I could actually undertake. I began to see that I could, and would, be able to provide unconditional love to others the way my friends had for me.

🌱 🌱 🌱

It was a hot morning in June 1967, and I was less than a year away from ordination when Shayla asked me to drive her to the airport. School was out for the summer break, and she was heading home to Texas to visit her family for a month. I was working at my dad's shop for the summer, and he let me have time off to drive Shayla to Los Angeles International Airport.

I picked Shayla up in my old, beat-up Chevy, and she kind of patted the side of the beast's door as she got in. There was no air-conditioning, and she rolled her window halfway down. My window was down all the way, and as we accelerated onto the freeway the wind noise became too loud to talk, so I rolled my window up. Shayla kept hers open, and she began talking about her family as we drove down the freeway. She was looking forward to seeing them again.

"Tell me about your mother," I said. "Funny, but you never talk about her. What's she like?"

Looking back on it, I can't believe I asked this question. If I'd been more intuitive, I should have put two and two together by that point in our friendship.

Shayla grew quiet in an instant, and all we heard for several miles was the rush of wind through the Chevy's window, the hum of the freeway under the tires. I got to thinking that maybe she hadn't heard me over the noise, so I decided not to press the point and rolled my window down all the way to let the breeze blow freely through. We drove like that, neither of us talking, all the rest of the way to the airport.

When we got to the terminal I broke the silence and offered to go inside with her, but Shayla said no. She insisted I drop her off at the curb. We parked in the congestion of the unloading zone, and I turned off the ignition. I was just about to climb out and get Shayla's bags when she put her hand on my arm and said, "Wait a minute."

She was looking straight ahead, and I was worried that a security guard would tell us to move along, but I had the presence of mind to ask, "What's going on, Shayla?"

She took a long swallow, paused, and said, "I was in seventh grade, Norm. We were coming back from a ball game, and a farmer's truck pulled out in front of us. Mom was driving. My little brother Keevin was sitting next to her in the front seat. Marge's sons, Bobby and Greg, were with us." Shayla stopped. Her voice crackled, her throat went up and down a couple times, and then she continued.

"It all happened so fast. There was no time to stop or swerve. Bobby and Greg were okay. I was shaken up, but physically okay. The gear shift went through Keevin's chest, so it was pretty serious for him, but he lived."

I asked my next question slowly. "Your mom?"

Shayla said nothing more. She squeezed her eyes tightly closed. And then she was crying.

I pulled her close and held her that way. Minutes ticked by. My embrace was pure, and all I wanted to do was comfort this girl, this friend who'd come to mean so much to me. I stroked her hair. Shayla cried in my arms. She had opened up worlds of new life for me, and yet she had already experienced so much pain herself.

Shayla's mom had been killed on impact. I began to see through a small window into Shayla's respect for big, safe cars. Shortly after the memorial service, Shayla's dad had sent her, not yet thirteen, from Texas to Long Beach to live with her older sister, Marge, and Marge's husband and family.

Shayla's two youngest brothers stayed with their dad, but the father figured that Shayla needed some womanly influence in her upbringing. Her dad never remarried.

In the aftermath of her tears, I started the car and drove around the airport loop, parked the Chevy in the lot, and walked Shayla inside the terminal. I carried her bags and made sure she found the right gate. There were no metal detectors or elaborate security procedures in those days, and Shayla gave me a long hug good-bye. In silence, I walked back to my car. We'd see each other soon. A month wasn't too long for us to be apart, was it?

Driving home alone, I thought about death, something I hadn't experienced much personally. I was too young to really understand much about it, although I knew it could really affect the loved ones who were left behind for a long time.

Other than my grandparents' passing, I had had only one significant brush with death. When I was sixteen, I knew a kid at school named Michael Gray. He was a grade lower than I was, and we weren't close, but he was a nice kid and I'd talked to him a few times. His dad had given him a model airplane with a working motor and steel wires to guide its flight. It was really cool. Honestly, I was a bit jealous of that plane.

One day I walked outside the school and saw Michael flying his plane toward the north end of the campus. He was only about fifty feet away from me and flying his plane near the entrance of the school where some big power lines crossed the property. I started to shout but already I was too late. The plane flew straight into those lines. A bolt of lightning flashed down the controller wires and blasted into his body. I heard a huge *kaboom*, and the boy caught on fire. I sprinted toward him. All of us did. Underneath Michael's feet a crater had been formed in the ground, a shallow hole about six inches deep, created by the explosion.

The hospital was directly across the street from the school. Michael lived a few days, and then he died. Seeing that boy go like that made me realize a person's life could end at any moment. I was rattled by the accident. Shaken. The only time I wanted my life to end was after I'd grown old. I'd be surrounded by family and friends. A life filled with accomplishments. Close to God. I'd go peacefully, maybe in my sleep. I couldn't imagine those closest to me ever dying. I couldn't imagine them dying back when I was sixteen when Michael had died. I couldn't imagine them dying even in my mid-twenties when Shayla told me about her mother. But it was true. Someday they'd all be dead. My parents. My brothers and sisters.

Shayla.

❦ ❦ ❦

As I was driving back from dropping Shayla off at the airport, a distinct feeling hit me—and it came with the force of a freight train. I was on Sepulveda Boulevard, heading back to the freeway, and I tried to put words to this intensity, but it was so unlike anything else I'd ever experienced that I couldn't.

Sure, I was feeling bad about Shayla's mother dying, and my heart filled with a new understanding of Shayla's grief and her response to it, but at least I had a category for those feelings, as difficult as it was to hear Shayla tell of it. No, this feeling wasn't about that. And it wasn't just feeling blue because I'd be without her for four weeks. It was something completely different. It was so foreign, like no force I'd ever encountered. At first it felt like an emptiness inside of me; a barren, gaping hole. Yet I didn't feel cold or scared, and the force didn't hurt me in any way. This feeling was warm. Happy. Paradoxical. Content, yet daunting.

I pulled my Chevy over and turned off the ignition. Around me were stores and restaurants and people walking up and down the sidewalk. It was just another busy day in Los Angeles. I needed to get back to my dad's shop, but I needed to concentrate intently on what I was feeling. Work could wait a few moments. I desperately needed to figure out what was going on inside my head.

Out loud, I said, "This is crazy. Norm, you are absolutely crazy. This will never work. Not in a million years."

And then I named the feeling.

I named it in surprise. But I named it honestly. I named it for myself to know so I could imbed it in the depths of my soul. After I named it, I had no doubts that the name was correct. I'd never felt so empty in all my life. I'd never felt so heavy. I'd never felt like I was missing someone more than I did at that moment. For the first time ever, I realized there was a void in my life. A huge void. And I had no conclusions yet what to do about this. I knew only of its existence. Shayla was gone. Not gone in death, but just gone to visit her family. And I couldn't handle being away from her. Not in this moment, not ever in my lifetime.

The feeling was this: When it came to Shayla Strohmeyer, I, Norm Supancheck, knew without a doubt that I was in love.

CHAPTER 4

What Would We Do?

It cost big money back then to call someone long distance on the phone, money I didn't have, and calling someone long distance just wasn't done that often. Those were the days long before Skype or Facebook. So I just counted the days for Shayla to come back from Texas. I counted, and I counted, and I counted. She sent me a postcard with a picture of a cactus and a cowboy hat on the front. I sent her one with a picture of the Santa Monica Pier. And time passed slowly. Very, very slowly. I worked each day at Dad's shop. I went to Mass. I hung out with Danny, Gabe, and Peter a bit. But mostly, I waited.

In four weeks' time I drove to the airport again, this time to pick up Shayla. I felt happy at the prospect of seeing her again, but nervous on the way over too. My whole body was tight, like I was being squeezed by a vise in my dad's metal shop, and the insides of my stomach pinged away like a pinball machine with a high scorer operating the paddles.

Running through my head was a jumble of emotion and thoughts. I couldn't begin to sort out what I was thinking or feeling. All I knew for sure was that I had missed Shayla a lot. I wondered if she had missed me as much as I'd missed her. I knew she'd missed me *some*—but I didn't know the degree of that missing, and I wondered if what she felt for me was anywhere close to what I felt for her.

Heck, I missed everything about Shayla. I missed our conversations when we were together. I missed her way of understanding things. I missed her beautiful way of seeing the world. Maybe she had received some strong feedback from her family while she was gone. Maybe they'd told her it was foolish to have grown so close to a young man who was heading for the priesthood. Maybe she'd come back and say, "Well, nice to know you, Norm. Have a swell life." Maybe she found somebody else, some Texas roughrider, and was now head-over-cowboy-boot-heels in love with him.

The questions banged against my head like a kick from a bull. What was it going to be like, seeing Shayla again after this important month apart? What would she say? What would she do? What was going to happen? What would our future be like? Could we really make this work? And what exactly was the "this" that I wanted to make work?

I parked my Chevy, walked briskly inside, found the correct gate, and bustled my way over to wait for Shayla's plane to land.

The first few people off the plane looked bedraggled and tired, like people always do when they've been on a flight. A few more passengers walked up the ramp and into the waiting room. A businessman in a suit. A hippy with a tie-dyed shirt and baggy jeans. A young mother with bags under her eyes, gripping the hands of her two children. Another string of strangers followed. I wondered if maybe Shayla hadn't boarded the flight. Maybe she'd decided to stay in Texas. Maybe she was sick. Maybe something was wrong.

And then she appeared.

She was midway down the ramp still gleaming, within a pack of people. She wore a short, striped skirt with a solid yellow top and a matching band in her hair. Her countenance was cool and fresh, like she'd just stepped out of an open-air café in Southern France. She spotted me and waved, then ran forward when the pack cleared, and we hugged for a long time.

"I missed you so much," I said.

"I missed you too," she said.

It was dinnertime, so we found her luggage at the baggage claim, then hopped in my car and cruised to a restaurant. I don't remember the name of it. It was a fancy joint somewhere along Sepulveda Boulevard. I don't recall what we ordered or even if I ate a bite. All I remember were the words of our conversation. I remember them precisely. A single question was on the tips of both of our tongues. Shayla was always very direct, and she articulated the question first. Her words that evening are seared into my brain forever. I repeated to her that I had missed her so much.

"I missed you very much also," Shayla said. "Do you want to marry me then?" Shayla wasn't proposing to me. She was seeking clarification.

"Yes." I uttered the word boldly. "I'd love to spend my life with you. But here's the problem, and I know I don't need to spell it out for you. I've been eleven years in the seminary now. I'm less than a year away from ordination. I don't know what God wants for us in this situation."

"That's a good question, Norm. We need to search out what God wants, because if we don't do what God wants then we're not going to be happy."

"What about you, Shayla?"

"I'd love to marry you too." She tucked a wisp of hair behind her ear and looked straight at me. She spoke her words decisively and clearly, like there was no hesitation in her mind, and she added, "I'd love to have a family with you. I'd love to grow old with you. I'd love to spend the rest of my life with you."

Those were the words I'd longed to hear. I hadn't even articulated them to myself quite like that, but Shayla had such a fine way of putting things into perspective. I felt exactly the same way about her. But I still had a question, and I found my tongue for this.

"What should we do then?"

That was the big inquiry, wasn't it: What was next? We were both silent for some time. The words we'd just spoken stretched out in front of us, audacious and momentous on the horizon. We couldn't take back those words now, even if we'd wanted to. We couldn't stuff that inquiry into some hidden place within us anymore, and how we dared answer that inquiry would determine the rest of our lives. I certainly had no answer. I was completely torn. I knew I wanted to become a priest. And I knew I wanted to spend my life with Shayla. I couldn't do both.

Again, she spoke first. "I think we just need to keep doing what we're doing, Norm. And let's pray about it. You go back to seminary. I'll go back to teaching, and then we'll talk about it after a while. In the meantime we'll pray specifically that God will either guide us together or guide us apart."

I nodded.

So this was it. The clock was now ticking toward my ordination date. That was our deadline. I drove her home and helped carry her bags inside. I gave her a little hug and kiss good night. I was so happy that Shayla was home. Everything felt the same again. Shayla was close by—near to me, close to my heart. With her in my life I felt within me an open wound close up and the ache go away, an ache that I'd never known existed before now. At the same time I felt vulnerable, susceptible to change. Like my life was a thousand-piece jigsaw puzzle lying on a coffee table out in the open. The picture was complete but so fragile. At any moment the pieces could separate. The puzzle would need to go back in the box.

❧❧❧

Late the following Friday afternoon, Danny came by the sheet metal shop. It was right around closing time, and he said hi to my dad, then just sort of hung around while I finished making an elbow for a downspout. It was a complicated piece, bent at eighty degrees, and I crimped the last part, soldered the joint and sanded the edges smooth, then swept up, washed and wiped my hands, and tossed a rag at him.

"Burgers?" I asked. Shayla was having dinner out with her sister that night.

Danny gave a little wince and shook his head. This surprised me. He was never one to shy away from food.

"Need to talk to you, Norm," he said. "Want to take a drive?"

I nodded. I could see something was chewing at Danny's insides. He had a river of information he needed to spill but he didn't know where. We hopped in my Chevy and hit the main drag, heading toward the beach. The sun beat down on us, even though it was nearing seven o'clock. My stomach growled.

"You know I've been seeing Lizzie a lot lately," Danny said, and then paused, like he was still thinking about how to articulate what he wanted to say next.

I nodded. Something had sparked to life inside of my friend those months ago when we first met Shayla at the conference. He'd never dated a girl before in his life, but after he met Shayla, it seemed like he was wide open to the whole concept of dating. His blood ran warmer. He never tried to date Shayla after that night when his car didn't start and I'd escorted her to the dance. But soon he met another girl—that much I knew. I'd been hanging out with Shayla so much that Danny and I had lost track of each other's daily routines.

"I've grown to love Lizzie," Danny added all at once. "I'm going to marry her."

My mouth fell open. I pulled my car over to the side of the road and shut off the engine. A hundred questions rose within me.

"It's true," Danny added. "I already told the rector I'm dropping out of seminary."

"When?"

"Lizzie and I don't have a date yet. But it'll be soon. Norm, I love her. I want to spend the rest of my life with her. Surely you can understand."

I managed a nod, but the news hit me hard. Hearing it directly from Danny's mouth like that sounded so stark. So irrevocable. Danny was leaving to start a different life. He was quitting the calling. Sure, I could understand why, but this felt so real. Not hypothetical. Danny would never become a priest.

Danny and I had become great friends, and I'd always thought he would make the ideal priest. I'd dreamed of both of us serving God together and sharing the good and bad things that we would go through in our callings. A few weeks earlier, my friend Peter had been told that he would not be ordained at the same time as the rest of us. School officials wanted him to wait and discern some more about his future. Another friend, John, who I'd grown up with in Long Beach, had also recently dropped out. With this news now of Danny's departure, I was beginning to feel scared. In my mind, they were all so good and so smart and so holy. I didn't think I measured up to their abilities. But if they could not be ordained, then who was I to be chosen by God? I was still too introverted, too shy to be a good priest. The only close friend still with me in the program was Gabe. At least the two of us would continue as friends and share with each other our successes and failures, our accomplishments and problems. I especially would miss Danny.

"Say something," Danny said. "Say anything."

But I couldn't. Not just yet. I kept quiet, and we sat like that for a few more minutes. We were closer to the beach now, and the air was cooler. A distinct smell of salt floated in through the open windows along with the breeze. Finally I said, "What will you do now for a career?" It was all I could think to ask.

"I'm not sure yet," Danny said. "I'm thinking about getting my MBA and going into business. But I don't know."

The change in career was only part of the adjustment Danny would need to make. Our undergrad college degrees would be recognized and would transfer pretty much anywhere. But most of the last three years we'd spent in seminary wouldn't transfer anywhere except to the priesthood. That meant Danny would need to start a new graduate program from scratch. At the very least it meant lost time and money out the window. The life skills we learned in the seminary would be valuable, sure, and the course content we'd studied would be useful many places in life. But from a schooling perspective alone, Danny's decision was huge.

I inhaled sharply and managed a smile. "I guess I need to say congratulations."

"Thanks," Danny said. "You'll come to the wedding, of course?"

I turned, grinned, and slugged Danny in the shoulder. Not hard. But just to let him know that he could count on me. "Wouldn't miss it for the world," I replied.

Danny shook his shoulders a bit, and I could see the tension had drained out of him. "By the way," he said almost as an afterthought. "How are you and Shayla doing?"

Well, I didn't know how to answer that. The news of my friend's upcoming marriage was still too monumental in my mind. How could I begin to tell Danny that Shayla and I were contemplating the very same thing?

"You feel like that burger yet?" I asked.

Danny grinned and nodded. He let his question lay unanswered.

I started my car and pulled out in traffic. At first, everything still felt the same. My close friend and I were still driving toward the beach. It was still nearly seven o'clock on a warm summer night in Los Angeles. But everything felt different too. My best friend had just made the biggest decision of his life. I would soon need to do the same.

⚜ ⚜ ⚜

Shayla and I saw each other a lot over the last few weeks of summer. We saw each other as much as we could, in fact. I worked all the time at the shop, and she volunteered helping kids, so our time together was here and there, except for the retreats. But each moment was treasured. We didn't talk further about our plans at first. We just had dinner at Denny's together, like always. Or we found some park somewhere and went for a walk. I held her hand a lot then. I held it every chance I got.

Fall came, and school started. It was my last year at the seminary. Everything felt different without Danny and John there. Shayla went back to teaching. My ordination was set for April 27, 1968, at the end of the school year. I prayed about the big decision in front of me, sure. I prayed about it all the time. I studied the Scriptures. I listened for God's voice. Nothing seemed clear.

Toward the end of October, Shayla and I met for our big talk. Enough time had passed that we needed to bring up the subject again and get it on the table so we could compare notes. We met at our favorite restaurant. We ordered cheeseburgers and fries, Cokes, and ice cream sundaes for dessert. But I picked at my plate, not diving in like I usually did. Shayla picked at hers too. My skin grew sweaty, and I had a heavy feeling in my stomach. As usual, Shayla led the conversation.

"Norm," she asked. "Did God answer your prayers?"

"No," I said. "I still don't know what to do. How about you?"

She turned quiet, and I heard the clanging of silverware off in the distance, like somebody had dropped a fork on a tile floor. I heard the bustle of waitresses bringing trays of food out of the kitchen and the chatter of restaurant patrons all around us. Into that backdrop of quiet chaos, Shayla spoke. "God answered my prayer," she said, "but I don't like what God said to me. He said we could have a wonderful life together. You'd make a wonderful husband, Norm. A wonderful father to our children. But I believe God is calling you to something bigger than our marriage."

"What could be bigger than our marriage?"

"God doesn't want you to be the father to one family, Norm. He wants you to be the father of many families." She paused and added, "That's what God told me."

I let her words sink into my mind, then blurted, "But God didn't tell *me* that."

Shayla smiled. This was not the conversation I wanted to be having. She reached over and took one of my hands in both of hers. She ran her fingers lightly along my hand and gazed at my fingers. She wasn't breaking up with me. She wasn't ending anything. There was too much warmth in her words still. She was simply relaying to me what the Spirit of discernment had spoken within her. Her words had been genuine when she said she wanted to marry me. I had no doubt of them. But she was listening to a higher calling. She was willing to sacrifice what she wanted for the sake of what she believed would be the best, because it would be what God wanted for both of us.

"We need to keep praying, Norm," Shayla said. "We need to keep praying that God will guide us. You're getting close to becoming a priest. I'll wait for you."

"How—" I faltered for my next words. "Exactly how will this work?"

Shayla's tone turned decisive as she unfolded a plan she had clearly thought through. "I won't date anyone until the matter is firmly decided. If you leave the seminary, then we'll get married. If you go through with the ordination, I will go to your ordination and then I'll begin dating again."

"That seems fair," I said, almost choking on the words, but truly I could see that it was fair and right and sensible and would give us time to be sure of our course, one way or the other. I looked at her for a long moment.

One long moment in time.

We ate our burgers then. We ate our fries and drank our Cokes. A while after the dinner plates were cleared the waitress brought us our ice cream sundaes. Shayla and I talked about only small matters then. About a movie she had seen. About a book I had read.

It wasn't over. The question still hung in the air. I wanted to marry Shayla. And I wanted to become a priest.

What would we do?

CHAPTER 5

Staring at the Sun

FROM THE TOP OF THE HILL where I walked, I could look out and see how I imagined the future to look. Acres of orange groves and lemon trees—leafy, lush, stretched out before me. One day homes would be built on these hills, homes with families living in them, all surrounded by music and laughter, wine for happiness and bread for sustenance. Grandparents. Fathers and mothers. Children. The path underneath my feet would be paved one day too, I imagined, but for now it was hard-baked clay. I kept walking and walking, praying and praying, looking out at the sky and the land and the life all around me, seeing birds flying, rabbits and squirrels feeding, praying with my eyes open, praying, praying, walking, walking. Far in the west toward the Pacific Ocean, the sun was setting, golden and blinding, and when I walked in its direction, I was encompassed by its rays.

The path on which I walked went all the way around the seminary grounds. Often I prayed in the chapel on campus, but sometimes I needed to be outside to communicate in a different way with God. The seminary was built on top of a terrace that overlooked farmland and orchards of avocados, oranges, and lemons. Decades earlier, a deep-pocketed city father named Juan Camarillo had donated the land. He and his brother Adolfo were horse breeders and ranchers. Thanks to hard work and an inheritance from their father, they became two of the principal property owners in Ventura County near the beginning of the twentieth century. Juan Camarillo had envisioned a school on the hilltop of his land that would one day train men of God. I was now walking the perimeter of the grounds of the school he'd envisioned, and as I walked, I wondered if my dreams too would someday come true.

One of those dreams would, I hoped, I guessed, and one of them wouldn't. And that was what I continually prayed about.

Father, in every generation You provide ministers of Christ and the Church. I come before You now, asking that You would give us priests who will lead and guide Your people. Raise up ministers who are generous in their service, willing to offer their lives and all their gifts for Your greater glory and the good of Your people. Amen.

The chapel was best for prayer in the early mornings and quiet evenings. I sat or knelt, and the early light shone through the stained glass windows and created a spectrum of blues and purples and yellows and reds. All was quiet in the chapel, peaceful and still. I simply tried to put myself into God's presence. There, I would find a voice amid the quietness. I would put away any bothersome thoughts. Whatever else was filling my mind—my studies, my weekend work at the metal shop, any concerns about my friends or family members—I'd set that aside so I could focus on God and incline my heart to hear His voice.

Father, what should I do? I love Shayla. You know that. I long to give my life to her in marriage. But what I long for most is for Your will to be done, as it is in heaven. I need wisdom, Father. I need Your guidance. I need Your voice alone. What should we do? For the sake of Your name, amen.

I believed that God was guiding me *because* of my prayers, and, strange as it felt in my mind, I believed that God was guiding me *in spite* of my prayers. The guidance was happening either way. I sensed that God was guiding me because of His character as a good shepherd. He was guiding me because of who He is, and the guidance was happening whether I asked for it or not. It would be mine for the taking if in faith I believed. As I searched for confirmation, I listened to what the peace inside my heart was telling me. I trusted that if I was in the wrong place or heading toward the wrong direction, then I wouldn't feel peace inside. I reminded myself of the words of Psalm 23. *The Lord is my shepherd. I shall not want. He makes me lie down in green pastures.*

He leads me beside still waters. What else does a shepherd do, I asked myself, except care for and guide his sheep?

My schedule was busy, and so was Shayla's. Yet she and I still went out during this extended time of consideration. We still talked. We still ate at Denny's. I still looked into her eyes and imagined the future like I had imagined it from the top of that hill.

In January 1968, Shayla and I drove again to her favorite spot overlooking the ocean. It was colder now, with a winter wind blowing fiercely on our faces off the water, and we grasped hands at the start of the trailhead and hiked to the rock on the cliff overlooking the sea.

In front of me was the same scenic outlook I'd seen so many months earlier on our first outing, the night of the middle school dance, the same waves and breakers crashing on rocks. But this time I found my gaze pulled away from the scenery. Now I could only look at the woman beside me, at how warm she was, how alive. When I studied her, I saw only beauty. Far away, so far away, was the image of my dorm room back at the seminary, as unembellished as a hard-backed chair, so stark in my mind now, so cold. Why would any man ever head in the direction of the priesthood, I asked myself, when he could be standing next to the welcoming warmth of such an incredible woman?

Our breath hung misty in the cold air, and as I stood next to Shayla with our hands entwined, I kept praying, praying, praying. Far in the west toward the Pacific Ocean the same sun I saw when I walked at the seminary grounds was setting, and when I broke my gaze from Shayla and stared in its direction I was staggered by its glory. The sun blazed in its brilliance, even far away as it was. Its rays broke through any grayness and coldness we were feeling and reached us where we stood. I considered the enormity of the sun, what a symbol it was of otherworldliness. I contemplated its transcendence and immanence—these characteristics of being both far away yet intimately involved in the affairs of mankind at the same time. This massive flaming star seemed so big, but it was merely a flyspeck in the vastness of God's universe.

I revered the sun as I stared at it because it was large and glorious—but that was only a reminder to me that God was infinitely larger and more glorious still. When I thought about all this, when I prayed through these ideas in my mind, I wasn't sure if I could admit my conclusions out loud yet, but I knew I was beginning to answer my own difficult question.

The answer was this: It was when, and only when I fixed my eyes on that which was incomparably glorious, and kept my eyes from swerving to the right or the left, that I could possibly head toward my destiny.

🌿 🌿 🌿

Back at my dorm room, alone, I flipped through catalogues. Even though the big decision—the question of whether to marry Shayla—was yet unsettled, I still needed to select a chalice. It was time. All my twenty-one classmates were doing it, and I was behind the curve. The chalice, to a priest, is like a briefcase to a businessman. He owns it. He keeps it close. He treasures its contents. Yet it's far more.

I flipped page after page, studying the myriad of designs available. Nothing looked right. I mulled all that my chalice would mean to me—if indeed I went ahead with my ordination in three months' time. The chalice is the cup that holds the wine of the Eucharist. It's a drinking goblet that's filled and refilled with the holiest of all drinks. Each time a priest celebrates Mass, he takes with him his own, personal chalice. He holds it in front of him and above him, arms outstretched to heaven, and his chalice acts as the container for the conduit of blessings between God and man.

I knew a chalice needed to be special. I knew that each time the wine was consumed, I would need to remind the people in my care that Christ died and gave His blood for us. I would inform them of what that death means to them, even today. I would tell them how a faultless man once took all the scourging of mankind's sin upon himself. He felt every murder. He felt every rape. He was robbed of all He valued. He took all destruction and tears and mourning and death. And He did that willingly, because of love. It was a massive love, I would tell them. An unending love. The kind of love that so loves the world that it holds forth an offer: eternal life to all who believe.

Just before Valentine's Day I drove home for the weekend to be with my family. Mom asked me if I'd picked a chalice yet. I shook my head no. Everybody in the family was home that weekend, and we came together in the living room and someone said, "What if we make Norm's chalice?" And someone else said, "How do you do that?" and I said, "I don't know, but I like that idea"—this idea of the people who'd known me longest coming together and creating something so personally valuable to me. We could all have input. I trusted their wisdom and creativity. I trusted their love. It seemed so right. I didn't have the heart to reveal my uncertainties. It seemed like the natural progression of things continuing to unfold.

Still, we needed wisdom, even to know how to craft such a vessel. So I prayed that if God wanted us to make my chalice, then He would show us that this creative process was part of His pathway for us. I heard about a Sister up in Palos Verdes who made chalices. She belonged to a small community, maybe four Sisters total, so I called her up and said, "I know you make chalices, but what we'd like to do is make our own. Can you show us how?" She agreed.

The Sister had a little shop up there, so we bought a flat piece of silver and took it to her shop. My family came with me, and we cut it out and heated it, then all took turns pounding it out to make the cup. We put little dings in it to make it look handmade.

Ideas came from my brothers and sisters. The base of the chalice was made in the form of a cross. My brother John had that idea. My sister Doris had the idea that part of the base could be made out of copper. She'd worked with copper once in a class at school, so she took copper and melted red glass on it, and that represented the blood of Christ. We fastened a silver piece on the bottom, and my sister Phyllis put the name of Christ on one side and my name on the other side to symbolize that I would always need to represent Christ.

For the inside of the cup, we wanted to use gold, but gold cost big money. We prayed about God's provision. Through my hobby of model rocketry, I had a connection at a nearby naval base, Port Hueneme. They used gold in the wiring for satellites so the lines didn't corrode, and they had some old satellite wire they gave us. We were able to extract the gold from the wire, and it was just enough for the inside of the cup.

Mom gave me both her wedding ring and her engagement ring, and we took the main diamond out to make another ring for her with stones representing each of her seven children. Then we took her original rings and fashioned a cross piece on the chalice. Then we took the wedding band left by my grandmother to form the leg of the cross, so the rings carried the blessings of a long heritage with them.

When it was finished, I liked the way my chalice looked, but it was so much more than simple admiration for an artifact. So many people I cared about had helped fashion this important vessel. I felt the opposite of abandoned, whatever that was. Supported, I guess. Surrounded by love. Seeing the pride, craftsmanship, and value placed into that chalice was an indication of honor. It felt like my close family was going to accompany me in this journey forward. The chalice was a reflection of the care of so many people who had helped me come so far in the journey toward becoming a priest.

I never wanted to let it out of my sight.

☙ ☙ ☙

On several evenings as I was out praying and walking, I must admit I thought about the question of sex, sure. Was this a big decision? Yes. As a young man, I was in the time of my life where I had strong sexual urges. I wanted to be with a woman. Certainly, I had these feelings. I knew if I became a priest, then I would need to let go of something I would love to have had in my life. I wondered how a young man could ever give up something so important. It seemed so impossible.

As I walked one evening around the campus, I was praying to God, and then I was silent. Into my mind rushed the story of Saint Peter on the Sea of Galilee. He's out there one stormy night with his friends. The words and story from Scripture I'd heard a thousand times before. I turned it over and examined it from all sides.

For a few hours Jesus had left his disciples, the young, straggling band of mostly fishermen who followed him. Jesus had gone up on a mountain by himself to pray. I could identify with that. While Jesus was praying, the disciples hopped in a boat, struck oars, and headed out across the sea, bent for the other side.

While out on the water, a wind arose. A wild wind. By then it was late in the evening, and the boat was a long way from shore. The disciples strained against the oars. They sweated and they stressed and they gritted their teeth in fear. They envisioned a capsized boat, I imagined, and the weight of the water pulling them down to the depths.

And then—suddenly, miraculously—Jesus was there. Walking toward them on the whitecaps. The disciples were afraid at first, thinking it was a ghost.

"Take heart!" Jesus called out. "It's Me. Don't be afraid."

Peter answered first. "Hey Jesus, if that's really you, then tell me to walk on the water too, and I'll come to where you are." Or words to that effect.

"Come on over," Jesus called out. A wave rushed at him and burst, showering him with a spray of water.

So Peter did. I could see it in my mind's eye. Peter, always headstrong and reckless in spirit, bounded out of the boat and started walking on top of the water toward Jesus. One step. Two. As long as he kept his eyes firmly fixed on the Son of God, he was okay. Three steps all in a hurry. Four—five—six—seven—eight. And then Peter stopped walking, suddenly realizing the impossibility of what he was doing. It was then, and only then, that Peter started to sink.

"Lord!" Peter cried out. "Save me!"

Immediately Jesus stretched out his hand and said, "Oh you of little faith. Why did you ever doubt?"

I could see that outstretched hand again. The hand that beckons toward what at first seems impossible. My decision toward chastity would not be made out of duty. It would be made in peace. A peace that overcomes fears. A peace that keeps one afloat on top of waves.

🌿 🌿 🌿

In the springtime of that year I traveled to Montezuma, New Mexico—a small, dusty town I'd wager would be difficult to find on any map today. I went there with my friends from Saint John's, Gabe and John. If we were headed toward the priesthood, then we wanted to become the best priests we could be, and that meant learning Spanish. Sixty percent of all Catholics worldwide speak Spanish, and a ton of them live in Los Angeles. We would need to learn this other language as well as we could so we could speak it, write it, think in it, bathe in it, even dream in it. Shayla was still ever present in my mind too. No, I hadn't forgotten her, but I needed to make this trip. I wanted to; I could feel this adventure's pull.

A seminary for Mexican students was situated in an old hotel that squatted near a hot spring just outside Montezuma. The hotel was a remnant of past glory and its paint was peeling now, its tiles chipped. The main buildings held forth towers and turrets and looked like a castle from a movie, but nothing was in good shape anymore.

The priests who taught there catered mostly to Mexican nationals who wanted to learn theology in the United States. About seventy seminarians were there—mostly younger guys like me. They took all their classes in Spanish—theology and preaching and philosophy. We attended classes with them, then interacted with them during the day. My friends from Saint John's and I vowed we'd speak nothing but Spanish the whole time we were there. None of the seminarians spoke English to us. We knew that would be the only way to learn.

It was rough in the beginning. Everything was a change. The school was so poor that they didn't eat any meat with meals. Meals were just rice and beans, beans and rice, a few tortillas, then more rice and beans. I'd learned some Spanish earlier in school, even minored in it in college, but I didn't know how to say a lot of things. All of us needed to learn very quickly. The phrase *Amo a una mujer. Yo amo a Dios* flitted through my mind on more than one occasion, although I never spoke it out loud. *I love a woman. I love God.*

On a Saturday morning, one of the students cranked up the engine to an old school bus they had on the grounds, and about forty of us jumped onboard for a sightseeing trip to nearby Albuquerque. It must have been nearly a hundred degrees already, and that old bus was a real rattletrap. They called it the "Lizard." With all the windows down, and no detectible shock absorbers so that all of us were bumping up and down in our seats, the bus backfired its way down the road, belching smoke every few seconds. We told jokes and sang songs and debated theology, all in Spanish, and we arrived in

Albuquerque, saw the sights, then boarded the bus for the trip back. Right in the middle of an intersection at busy cross streets, the school bus coughed twice and then sputtered to a stop. The driver tried to restart the bus, but that old ironsides had really given up the ghost. A few of us climbed out, opened the hood, and jabbered away in Spanish, wondering what to do. Traffic piled up behind and all around us. A policeman came along, his eyes narrowed, and yelled at us to "get that bus out of here!"

"*Cómo?*" one of the students asked simply. "How?" That bus was heavy as a tank.

We had a rope, so the policeman hooked it to his city pickup truck and tried to give the bus a tug. The rope broke, so we tied it in a knot and tried again. This time all of us climbed out and pushed all together, everyone shouting in Spanish, heaving, sweating, laughing. Inch by inch, the bus lumbered to the side of the road.

Through all of this, none of us had spoken a word of English. I felt immersed in the Hispanic subculture of our country. I felt how I imagined a priest in Los Angeles would feel.

To graduate from the language school, the three of us *Americanos* needed to put on a mock radio program done completely in Spanish, including sports, news, current events, jokes, and a play. We needed to talk quickly, fluently, and clearly in Spanish for an hour, all in front of the staff and all the other students. We put on our show, and when we finished, they clapped and cheered wildly. We knew that if we'd communicated well enough to elicit that sort of response, then we had arrived.

On the way home to Los Angeles, we stopped at the first diner we spotted so we could order meat. We craved steaks, but no steaks were to be had. The only thing on the menu was hamburgers. Hamburgers? I couldn't even remember how to say the word in English. I felt completely immersed now in my new world. When they were finally slung across the lunch counter at us, sizzling and cheesy, those hamburgers tasted better than anything I'd eaten in a long while.

❧ ❧ ❧

I'd seen ordination ceremonies before. I knew what they were like. Conceptually, being ordained into the priesthood could be compared to a cross between passing the bar for a lawyer and a coronation ceremony for a king. By the time a man has been ordained, he's gone through four years of college and four years of graduate school, all his studies, all his practicums, all his initial testing and exams, and now he's officially recognized in his new role. The ceremony itself acts as the dividing line. Before the ceremony, a man is still considered a student. After the ceremony, a man is a priest.

On April 27, 1968, seventeen seminary students gathered at Saint Vibiana Cathedral near the seminary for an ordination ceremony. It was a full house, absolutely packed, and a person needed tickets to get in.

The cardinal archbishop from the archdiocese of Los Angeles led the ceremony. The candidates started by lying on the ground with their faces toward the ground and their heads toward the altar. The act symbolizes unworthiness of the new role, a humility for this calling. The archbishop called upon the students to rise. He prayed, then read some Scriptures. The candidates went to where he stood and placed their hands on top of the open Bible. The archbishop commissioned the students to go forth and live the teachings of Scripture themselves, to preach the word of God faithfully, and to bring God's word and the ministry of Jesus to people everywhere. He then anointed their hands with oil as a sign that God wanted to bless the candidates and for them to use their hands to bless others. The archbishop laid his hands on their heads as a sign of God sending his Spirit to live in them. The candidates entered into the Eucharist celebration, the taking of the Body and Blood of Christ. They consumed the elements first themselves, then distributed the elements to their family members next, then to the rest of the people in the cathedral. There was a final blessing. A prayer. The ceremony was officially over. The candidates were ordained.

One of those candidates was me.

All through the ceremony, powerful feelings had pummeled me. Strongly, I felt God's call to be here, to be going through this ceremony, to be taking this next important step to officially become a priest. But in my heart I felt so unworthy. More than one hundred young men had entered the high school portion of seminary together. From that number, only eleven were ordained plus another six who'd joined us in later in college. Why was I one of the chosen ones? Many of those other students were smarter than I was, holier than I was, worthier than I was. Surely they would make better priests. So why did God insist upon choosing me?

Mixed with this deep sense of unworthiness came a feeling of excitement too. I'd agreed with God about this calling. I'd said yes to His invitation to help bring healing and wholeness to the world. It felt like a huge task, one that was far beyond my capabilities, yet I had the feeling I was joining a long line of people who'd faithfully administered this task. When the bishop laid his hands on my head, I felt like I was participating in an ancient and solemn rite—a baton was being passed to me in the marathon of all races. It was now my job to serve people in love. It was now my job to be present with people as they walked through life's most difficult seasons. I was to help bring God's blessings to the world, and somehow God had entrusted to me this most awesome of jobs.

Afterward, my family was first in line to greet me. I was happy in that moment. I was thinking only thoughts of God. One by one, my brothers and sisters hugged me. A string of relatives followed. Aunts and uncles. Cousins. Nieces and nephews.

My good friend Danny stood in the line to greet me. He stood along with his fiancée, Lizzie.

Somewhere near the middle of the line stood Shayla. She was smiling. Her heart was fully prepared, as was mine. We had made our momentous decision over such a long and careful time that when the cinch point came, it seemed like a thing we just eased into, and when her time came to greet me, she walked up and gave me a big hug. She whispered in my ear, assuring me that I would be a good father to many families. And if I remember this correctly, I'm almost positive that she reminded me again, just for good measure, she would start dating again soon.

The next day, as part of my new duties, I held my first official Mass in the parish. The Mass acts as a second part of the ordination process, even though a man is officially ordained by then. Again, I felt that strange mixture of unworthiness and great calling. Celebrating Mass had always been important to me. It was something I did nearly every day, and now here I was leading people in this same celebration. Except this time I wasn't in the pew anymore. I was up front, steering the ship. We held a reception in the hall afterward. Everybody was really happy.

Including me.

After that, we were given four weeks' vacation. My parents and I drove across country to see relatives in Arizona, Nebraska, Massachusetts, Rhode Island, and Maine. I remember I ate a lot of clam cakes in Cape Cod. My mom's relatives held a celebration for us over there. Turns out, those clam cakes were only the first course of that meal. I'd already eaten my fill, but then they brought out shrimp, and I ate a ton of those. Then fish, and I stuffed it in. Then they brought out lobster, and I said, "Oh my goodness." I was so stuffed I thought I'd burst.

I was set to report for duty as a priest on the first Saturday of June. I'd never lived in a rectory before, never performed a baptism, never led a funeral, never been called "Father," never counseled a married couple, never participated in the day-to-day running of a church, never done a lot of things a man of my new standing was expected to do, and I felt more than a twinge of apprehension at what lay before me. My interaction with Shayla had done wonders for my shyness, yet I was still essentially scared of people. All I'd known for the past twenty-one years was my schooling, but now my new life as a priest was set to begin.

When I got back to Los Angeles after the trip, I visited the seminary grounds one evening, late. I wasn't there to meet anyone. I was there to walk the path alone with God.

As I walked, I prayed, and I wondered in prayer if a man could actually fall out of love with a woman when once he's held her so close to his heart. I wasn't sure if I even liked that phrase—"fall out of love." I remembered how, months earlier, my sister-in-law had pulled me aside in the kitchen at Thanksgiving and warned me that I needed to be careful—for Shayla's sake as well as mine. The close relationship I had with Shayla was bound to end one of two ways, she'd insisted. We would either break up or get married. There were no other options.

As I walked that path, I knew firmly and irrevocably that the choice had been made, yes. Shayla and I would never be married. She was free to love again, and love deeply, and I knew she would. One day she would meet the love of her life, and it wouldn't be me. She was freed up to love her future husband and family wholeheartedly, and I knew she would embrace her new role with verve and delight, spirit, and abandon.

I, in turn, was freed up to live a life of service and sacrifice, a life that wasn't consumed with a family of my own. And no, I did not plan to spend the rest of my life pining in my heart for Shayla, for the woman I never married. I knew even then, that evening as I walked, that wouldn't be the case.

But with all due respect to my sister-in-law, and with the advantage now of decades of hindsight, I disagree.

I strongly disagree.

I can confidently state today that Shayla and I never broke up.

Never.

CHAPTER 6

What Have I Gotten Myself Into?

IN THE FIRST FEW WEEKS AND MONTHS after I was ordained, I continued to see Shayla at the Youth Encounter retreats and here and there, always in groups of people, never one-on-one. She had a ton of friends, and soon she moved out of her sister's house into her own apartment along with some other girls. That fall, Shayla began a master's program at Loyola Marymount University, so she was always busy. Still, she stayed true to her promise to herself and found time for dating. At first it was with nobody steady. She went out with this friend or that friend, and I felt okay about it. I truly did. It wasn't my place to feel anything else.

Once our decision was made, the struggle that had pulled me in such polar opposite directions seemed over, or at least that struggle gradually subsided. My feelings for Shayla didn't turn off, but seemed to be taking a new direction. Besides that, I was busy dealing with my own troubles. Right away I wondered if I'd made a mistake in becoming a priest.

Since I knew some Spanish, I was assigned to the Santa Isabel Parish in East Los Angeles, a blue collar, high-crime area of the city populated mostly by Hispanics and Hispanic gangs.

The day before I was set to report to the rectory (the house where priests live), I called the church to let the pastor know I was coming. Much to my surprise, the voice that answered the phone was female. She sounded elderly and she spoke loudly, almost shouting into the phone.

"HELLO. THIS IS SAINT ISABEL PARISH. WHAT DO YOU WANT?"

"This is Father Norm Supancheck. I've just been assigned to your parish. I wanted to let the monsignor know I'd be arriving tomorrow."

"NO . . . WE DON'T HAVE ANY FATHER NORM HERE. SORRY—I CAN'T HELP YOU."

"Yeah, I know. *I'm* Father Norm, and I'm coming tomorrow. To live there."

"I'M MRS. EVANS. THE HOUSEKEEPER. NO, WE DON'T HAVE ANY FATHER NORM HERE. YOU'LL HAVE TO TRY SOME-WHERE ELSE."

She was hard of hearing, I gathered. We talked for another five minutes, with me trying to explain who I was and why I was calling, but nothing was getting through, so I gave up.

The next day, just after suppertime, I drove over to East Los Angeles where the church was located on the corner of two main streets, Soto and Whittier. I'd never been to this area of town, and I counted four police cars and two fire engines on the way over. I found the church, parked my car on the street and got out, smoothed my suit jacket and adjusted my collar, and looked around. Near the church a lot of young people seemed to be just hanging around outside apartment buildings and stores, lounging on steps, smoking, or shooting the bull. Across the street was a bar with all kinds of noise coming out of it. Everywhere I heard Spanish. Summertime was arriving, and the day had been a scorcher, so people and noise and activity had moved outdoors. I walked to the front door of my new home and knocked.

A tall, stern-looking, gray-haired man slowly creaked open the front door. He looked me up and down, introduced himself as the monsignor, Father Sheehan, and said in an Irish brogue, "You must be Father Supancheck. I have been expecting you. Come in." There was no smile in his voice. Not a hint of warmth. Every movement he made was formal, and right away he led me upstairs to show me to my room. In addition to the elderly housekeeper, another priest lived in the rectory too, Father Javier Martiarena, and he and I would share a bathroom, said the monsignor. That was the extent of the tour.

"Tomorrow's my day off," the monsignor added, almost as an afterthought. "It's Father Martiarena's day off too. The housekeeper, Mrs. Evans, does not drive, so I'll be driving her over to her family's home for a visit."

"Who's going to be here then?" I asked.

He pointed a bony finger at me. "You." He turned on his heel and walked away. Our conversation was over. I still had a hundred questions running through my mind. I stood a few moments, unsure where to begin. It looked like I was to experience total immersion into my new work. Maybe that was a good thing for a young man who needed to deal with his feelings for a young woman. There didn't seem to be any place in the rectory for socializing with the people I now lived with, so I unpacked my things, read a bit, and went to bed.

That first night in East Los Angeles was a real eye opener for a kid from Long Beach. Sirens blared by the parish throughout the night. People yelled on the streets. I heard gunshots. There was no air conditioning in the rectory, so I needed to keep my window cracked so I wouldn't suffocate in the heat. All night I tossed and turned, feeling out of place and completely alone.

The next day dawned early. I showered, dressed, and went to the kitchen for breakfast, but nobody was there. I was too nervous to eat. There were no notes, no directions. I had no idea what to do. I went into the office area of the rectory, sat down, and stared at the phone. A clock on the wall ticked in my ears.

Sure enough, soon the phone rang. A woman asked me in Spanish what time Masses were going to be held the following Sunday. I said I didn't know. She asked to talk to a priest. I said I was a priest. "What kind of priest doesn't know what time the Masses are?" she retorted, and hung up. I looked all over for a bulletin or calendar that would give me information, but there was nothing.

An hour ticked by. I sat and stared at the phone.

A knock sounded on the front door and I ran to answer it. A whiskered man in a tattered coat stood before me, his palm outstretched. A panhandler. "*Tengo hambre,*" he said. "I'm hungry." I didn't know what to do. He stared at me a moment. I stared back. The stench of cheap wine wafted off his body.

"*Un momento,*" I said. I ran to the kitchen, hunted around for peanut butter and jelly, slapped together a sandwich, and brought it back to him at the door. He gave me a long, careworn glare, then took the sandwich and shuffled off down the street.

The phone rang again and I sprinted back to the office. The man on the other end was speaking Spanish so quickly I needed to ask him to slow down. I was fluent, but not that fluent. He slowed down long enough to utter two words, then sped right back up with a long blast of monologue. I heard "baby dedication" and "important" and "lots of people coming." I fished around for a pencil and scratchpad to take notes. He said *adios* and hung up before I got very far.

The phone continued to ring throughout the day. I continued to know nothing and misunderstand everything. People continued to knock on the front door. I was a disappointment to them all.

Late in the evening, the two priests and the housekeeper returned. The monsignor asked for a recap of the day but stopped me before long and shook his head with a frown. "Father Supancheck, I'm tired," he said. "I need to go to bed. We'll talk tomorrow." Just like that he was gone. The other priest was already in his room. The housekeeper was in hers.

I sighed and went to mine.

That second night was a similar cacophony of sirens, shouts, and gunshots. I slept maybe an hour. When I got up, I splashed cold water on my face and looked into the bathroom mirror. My eyes were bleary. My face haggard. *What have you gotten yourself into, Norm?* I asked myself. *Did you make a mistake?*

A rapid knock on the bathroom door interrupted my thoughts. "He-e-e-y, Father Norm, you done in there yet?" It was the younger priest, a Spaniard. "I got to do my beezness quick!"

✤ ✤ ✤

The next day after the Masses were over, the monsignor assigned me a new car, a ten-year-old Chevy. My other car, the '55 Chevy, was more of a family car, so I'd passed it along to my sister. Next door to the church sat Salesian High School, and the monsignor informed me my car was parked in the lot at the school. I walked over, found the car, climbed in, and turned the key. Not so much as a sputter. Upon opening the hood, I discovered no battery.

Three younger teens watched me this whole time. "Hey Father, you need a battery?" one said with a sly grin. "We can get you one."

One of the others winked. "Yeah, and cheap."

"Uh, that's okay," I said.

They looked disappointed. I bought a battery from a nearby auto parts store and installed it. The car rumbled to life.

I wish I could say the same about my new calling. We held six Masses per weekend, two in English and four in Spanish. Right away I was assigned to preach at two. Monsignor Sheehan was fluent in Spanish and very wise. People loved his homilies. Same with Father Martiarena. His speaking was smooth and loaded with solid content. Me? I stumbled over what to say and how to say it. Whenever I preached in Spanish I needed to stop every so often and ask the congregation how to say a certain word or phrase. I knew enough from my studies to be able to provide solid content, but I was so shy I had no dynamics in my communication. No delivery, no style.

The Sisters who taught at the school invited me over for dinner. "Father Norm," said one—and this is an exact quote—"your preaching is horrible. You are like an airplane that flies around without landing." She slapped a pork chop on my plate and smiled. "More peas?"

They weren't the only ones to notice.

I was invited to speak at a retreat for the students at nearby Don Bosco High School. I prepared some talks I thought would be good for the kids, but the speaking portion of the retreat went poorly. The students were whispering to one another. None listened. Some openly said they were bored. I went to a friend, Father Tom, who had great success working with youth, and asked him why I was such a failure. He got right to the point.

"You're too shy," he said. "You're letting your shyness inhibit you. Just say what you need to say. You talk with so much reticence that you don't sound like you even believe what you're saying. If you sound like you don't believe what you're saying, then none of the students will ever believe you either."

Father Tom was correct. After Mass one weekend, I figured I should stand outside the entrance of the church as everyone was walking out the door so I could shake hands and talk with the parishioners as they left. So I stood there, but nobody shook my hand. I overheard a couple say—and this is another exact quote, "This new priest looks nice, but he's just standing there with his hands in his pockets. Why doesn't he want to greet us?"

That was a clue. I was waiting for them to reach out. They were waiting for me. I took my hands out of my pockets and introduced myself to the couple. It was a start. But still I felt disoriented.

I was supposed to be part of the elementary school's life and functions next door. It was a Catholic school, and the administrators wanted someone to talk with the kids and say a blessing before lunch—that type of thing. But the kids took one look at me and wrote a note to the monsignor saying, "We don't want a gringo priest at our school." Another exact quote.

The neighborhood surrounding the parish was very much economically impoverished. During World War II, a central housing project had been built nearby called Estrada Courts, and over time it had become the headquarters of a gang, the Barrio Nuevo Estrada. Because the B and V sounds are close in Spanish, they called themselves the VNE for short. Various sub cliques existed within the gang, the Tiny Winos, the Devils, and the Malos, to name a few, and none of them were fooling around. They were known and feared for their drug deals, racketeering, extortion, fights, illegal betting, and, yes, murders.

My boss, Monsignor Sheehan, when he first came to L.A. as a young priest from Ireland, went to the bishop and said, "Give me the poorest parish you have." Back then, the area was called Simon's Brickyard because a lot of residents worked for a nearby brick-making plant. So the bishop gave him the area. Father Sheehan started out ministering to the laborers from the yard. He was able to build a small church. Then the freeways came through. They knocked down the church, so a new church was built, this one larger. He prayed a lot that a school could also be built because the government wasn't doing much at the time to provide schools in that area. One day a woman drove up and said to him, "God called me to start a school out here, but I don't know why." Father Sheehan said, "God sent you because I've been praying for it." So she started a school.

I was supposed to start a youth group at the parish, so I caught some kids after Masses and was able to gather eight of them. Their parents were all part of the parish. These were the "good kids" from church families. These kids were important to minister to, just as everyone is important, but already I had the good sense to know a priest should look for needs outside the walls of the church too. So I walked down the street one day, looking for teenagers I could invite to youth group.

The first bunch of kids I ran into comprised about nine youths, maybe aged fifteen to eighteen. They were all Hispanic boys, all dressed in baggy pants and T-shirts. All wore matching hats. I invited them to the meeting at the church the following Monday. At first they declined, but I was feeling tougher by then and was fairly frustrated with my ineffectiveness on the job, so I said, "Look, if you don't come, then I'm going to come looking for you." And I walked away.

The next Monday, the eight church kids from the parish gathered at the appointed time. I started the meeting, and about ten minutes later, the group of nine street kids showed up. We were sitting in a circle in the middle of a fairly good-sized hall. My regular kids took one look at the street kids and literally ran to the other side of the room.

I followed them and asked quietly, "What's the matter?"

"You know who they are, don't you?" one of my parish kids said, his lips trembling.

I didn't know. And I didn't care. They were here at youth group, and this was going to be fun. I led the church kids back to the circle and invited the street kids to sit down.

"Make me," said their leader. He was stocky and muscular, Mexican, one of the older ones.

I reacted on reflex. I'd grown to about six foot two inches tall by then, and I'd played my share of football back in high school. Thanks to working all those years in my dad's metal shop, my muscles were used to pounding metal all day long. "You want me to make you?" I asked. "Okay." I went up to the leader, grabbed his arms, and wrestled him to the ground. He fought back, but I quickly pinned him. He mumbled his consent, so I let him up and said, "Sit."

He sat.

And so did all the other kids in my new youth group.

We took it from there.

⚜ ⚜ ⚜

At a gathering of friends in June 1969, Shayla introduced me to a young architect named Dave Ebner. This was only a couple of years after the so-called summer of love in the parlance of the day, but he was the real deal. Dave was from Ohio and had come out to California to further his training and professional licensing credentials. Right away, Dave seemed like a swell guy. A shock of dark hair, a straightforward handshake. He'd done some bricklaying work before becoming an architect, and I knew any man who could lay bricks would be an honest, hardworking type of guy.

I noticed something different in the way Shayla looked at Dave. She'd introduced me to a few other guys she'd dated on and off, but around Dave there was a new quickness in her step, a lightness in her voice, characteristics she didn't exhibit around anybody else. Maybe not even me. For the time being, I put it out of my mind and went back to work.

My youth group was all over the place in terms of what they knew and didn't know. The parish kids had mostly grown up in church and were mostly well versed in spiritual matters. The street kids were as raw as could be and knew nothing. We started our meetings slowly, just with introductions and a few games. A short devotion or two. A bit of praying. Just the basics. The boys from the street started bringing their girlfriends, and pretty soon we had a good-sized group, about forty kids.

Plenty of these teenagers had never been outside their neighborhood, so I got permission to start doing retreats and outside activities with them. As a group, we went to the beach, to movies, to the mountains, on hikes. Any chance I got, I looked for windows into their lives to tell them about the love of God, about what He might mean to them, about how He could give them a hope and a future. Slowly they started responding. The group began to bond. The kid I'd once wrestled to the ground became a leader when it came to praying for others.

Another one of the guys, Julio, lingered after youth group one week. He was about sixteen, a smart kid, and always cracking jokes. Underneath his eye was the faint remnant of a scar.

"Father Norm," he said in Spanish. "How come you take us all these places like the movies and the beach? Nobody ever cares about us. Nobody ever takes us to these places. How come you do?"

"It's what I do." I shrugged. I wasn't positive how to answer his question.

"You know what?" He paused and gave a half sneer, half grin. "You're okay for a gringo."

After that, word got around the neighborhood that the gringo priest was okay. Slowly I started to feel accepted. I made a few close friends at the parish. The kids from the school next door changed their minds and wrote a new letter to the monsignor, saying it was okay after all if I led in prayer at lunchtime.

One day, about a year after I'd started the youth group, I was walking down the street when some residents stopped me and began to profusely thank me for what I was doing in the community.

"What did I do?" I asked. I genuinely didn't know.

"You've been working with the White Fence Gang," one woman said. "Those hoods were really terrorizing the neighborhood before you showed up."

The White Fence Gang? So that's who they were. I just thought they were some kids who needed a youth group. Some kids who needed to experience for the first time a tangible expression of the love of God. Even after I learned their identity, nothing changed between me and them.

Still, I deliberately didn't let these small successes go to my head. I considered myself a brand new priest. A newbie. A greenhorn. I was surprised one day when a call came into the parish from the Santa Fe Hospital, and Monsignor

Sheehan told me to take it. A man was in the hospital, dying. Monsignor Shee-han wanted me to learn the ropes, and this call seemed like a real boilerplate death. Recite the last prayers. Pray for the family. Comfort the grieving. All practical ministry actions I needed to learn by doing. "Send a priest quickly," the hospital administrator said over the phone. "He doesn't have long to live."

I hopped in my car and drove over to the Santa Fe Hospital. It was nicknamed the Railroad Hospital and was a small place over on South Saint Louis Street in the Boyle Heights neighborhood. Maybe seventy-five patients total. Sort of a dark place, older, creepy—it would make a good location to shoot a horror movie.

Sure enough, the man was barely breathing. His skin was pallid and pasty. He was hooked up to a dozen different tubes. He wasn't responsive to my voice or touch on his arm.

"Would you please pray for him?" asked an elderly woman. She clutched my arm tightly. "Pray that he'll live." It was his wife, and she collapsed in my arms, weeping. This was real life. I didn't learn any answers to this in seminary.

So I just sat with the woman for a while. I didn't know what else to do. I held her hand and read to her a few Scriptures. Then I anointed the man's forehead with the sacred oil I'd brought, and I prayed. While I was praying, a verse came to mind. James 5.16. "The prayer of a righteous man has great power in its effects." I'd always considered that verse more metaphorical than concrete. Still, I prayed that the man would be comforted in his affliction. That his spirit would be at peace. That his soul would be right before God. And, almost as an afterthought, I prayed for his healing.

When I left I said to the nurse, "Call me if there's any change." The nurse gave me a solemn nod. What I meant by that was, "Call me when he's dead." She was an old bird and knew the priestly lingo.

Early the next morning I drove back to the hospital. I hadn't received a call yet, but I was sure the man was dead by now. There was simply no way anyone in his condition could live through the night. I figured the hospital administrators were just waiting until a civil hour to call. I walked up the stairway to the second story to the man's room and peeked my head inside. His room was empty. No patients. No family members. No cards or flowers. I walked back out into the hall and found a nurse.

"What funeral parlor did they take his body to?" I asked.

The nurse shrugged. "A priest came yesterday and prayed for him. After the priest left, the man stood up and began to walk around. He said he'd never felt better, so he left."

🌿 🌿 🌿

Shayla continued to be one of the leaders at the Youth Encounter retreats, and I often saw her at those. But things between us were different now. I still loved her strongly, dearly, specially, but it felt somehow more like the love I felt for my sisters. It was a love of encouragement and support, of friendship and depth. I became better friends with David. He was a good guy, and he showed me a couple of the houses he'd designed and built. He had a real eye for craftsmanship. He was a true mechanical and engineering artist.

One day I was home alone at the parish when I heard a knock on the front door. When I opened it, Shayla stood there alone.

"Can I come in?" she asked. "I need to ask you something, Norm. It won't take long."

I nodded and led her into the kitchen. I could tell something heavy was on her mind, so without saying anything, I fixed her a cup of coffee and we sat at the table. As always, she got right to the point.

"Dave and I want to get married, and we want you to do the wedding. Will you?"

I took a very deep breath. I needed to think about that. Shayla kept her blue eyes firmly fixed on mine. She drummed her fingers on the table, waiting for the bottom line. In the space of the ten seconds of contemplation I allowed myself, a multitude of strong feelings coursed through my mind and heart. Who was I kidding? This was Shayla we were talking about here. She was as close as family. How could I even hesitate?

I swallowed and said, "I'd be honored. I wouldn't want anybody else to do it."

Shayla let out a little squeal. She stood up first, and I stood up, and she walked around the table to where I was and hugged me tight. She gave me a few more details and promised to call soon, then left. *That's it,* I thought as I closed the door behind her. *This is final.*

Later that evening I knelt beside my bed and tried to pray. In my core, I was all for the wedding. I knew they'd be perfect for each other. Still, Shayla's news landed so permanently in my gut. As permanent as my ordination did for her, I guessed.

Jesus, I prayed *You attended weddings, and you weren't the groom. You even turned water into wine at one of them. You celebrated these unions. Help me to celebrate this one. For the sake of my calling. For the sake of Shayla and Dave. Amen.*

On August 22, 1970, I presided over the wedding of Shayla Strohmeyer and David Ebner. I was twenty-eight years old, still a young man myself. I have pictures of the ceremony, but I don't remember a lot about it. Shayla was dressed in white from head to toe, and she carried a small bouquet of flowers. Dave wore a white tuxedo jacket with black pants. Shayla had on just a touch of makeup, and her smile all that day was genuine. When her father walked her down the aisle, Shayla was looking into David's eyes, not mine.

The service itself went well. It was fun actually. I got to meet members of both families—people I'd heard about for a long time but had never met.

After the reception, Dave and Shayla drove down the street heading toward their honeymoon and new life together.

When you care about someone, you want that person to be happy.

That was the feeling I decided to go with. I claimed that feeling in an intentional choice.

CHAPTER 7

When I Stopped Panicking

DAVE AND SHAYLA'S FIRST FEW MONTHS of married life seemed to go smoothly. They moved near enough to the rectory that we all saw each other fairly often—every couple of weeks or so. Theirs was a peaceful home, filled with love and laughter, wisdom and fun. Despite her busy schedule, Shayla still found time to plant a garden. She grew roses and lilacs, dahlias, and daffodils.

Right away, things went smoothly among all of us. I never sensed any jealously, tension, or weirdness. All three of us instantly morphed into great friends. Dave was helping out some colleagues with a building project in Anaheim and needed some sheet metal work done, so I steered him toward my dad's shop, which he readily used. Shayla continued to volunteer as a leader for Youth Encounter, and we still saw each other at retreats.

Dave had come from a large Catholic family himself, so he seemed appreciative of having a priest in his life. In retrospect, it even proved humorous a few times. Once, early in their marriage, Shayla and Dave got into a mild argument, as newlyweds are prone to do. I think Dave had come home after a long day of work and had one beer too many. They talked it out but couldn't reach a resolution, so Shayla said, "Let's let Norm decide." They called me.

"Shayla," I said. "Guys will be this way from time to time. There's a lot of pressure at work for Dave, and you just gotta understand guys. Give him some room. You still married a quality man. Don't worry. It'll all work out."

And it did work out. I tried never to take sides or drive a wedge between them. I always counseled them toward greater empathy with each other, greater communication, greater understanding. They never needed much help from me. Overall, Shayla and Dave enjoyed a healthy and harmonious marriage right from the start. They were right for each other. That fact seemed like another confirmation to me that Shayla and I had made the right choice those few years ago when we decided not to get married.

I wish I could describe my job as altogether healthy and harmonious. This necessary process of changing the world through love looked one way on paper, so purposeful and beckoning, yet an entirely different way in real life. While at Santa Isabel, I concluded that the real work of being a minister is to wade neck deep into the river of humanity's problems and conflicts. I didn't hope to swim against the current. Instead, I was caught right up in it, and I merely hoped to survive.

In the early 1970s, the racial tension in East L.A. crested the river's banks and became a flood. Most of the police who patrolled our area of the city were white, and most of the population was Hispanic. Overall, those were difficult days for the city, and the conflicts seemed to touch everybody in the neighborhoods I ministered in. Most of the kids I worked with weren't dangerous. They were just kids. They weren't hated by the police. They were simply unknown, and so they were feared. Very few, if any, authority figures were letting go of their fears so they could reach out and truly connect.

Within my group, I had lots of kids with nicknames. For instance, there was Flaco, Paco, Chino, the Ghost, and the Rat. I had plenty of other kids who went by their regular names: Pedro, Isabella, José, Maria, Juan, Rosa, and Geraldo. All the street kids wore white T-shirts and baggy pants and used all the cool Chicano street slang.

There was a municipal curfew then for teens, and the police stopped Pedro one evening and took him in. He was older, nearly eighteen, and when I visited the jail, Pedro's lip was cut, his eye puffy and dark. I asked him how this happened, and he didn't want to talk about it, but later in the conversation he whispered that the police had done it to him. I pressed Pedro hard, asking if he'd resisted arrest, but he swore he didn't. I prayed with him, promised to help him contact a lawyer, and said I'd go talk to his mother and see if I could smooth things over there. It was hard to discern the truth. But after these same kinds of injuries cropped up a few more times with several different older teenagers I knew, I began to grow suspicious of the authorities.

I don't mean to say that all the kids in my group were squeaky clean. They weren't. Some were genuinely troubled kids from genuinely troubled homes. A few were involved with drugs, stealing, or vandalism. There were problems at school, problems after school, problems at church, problems with their friends. Some slept around, seeking what they falsely equated with love wherever they could find it. There were fights within the gang culture. Lots of arguments, posturing, and threats.

I needed help, so I began to work closely with my old friend, Gabe, now a priest himself over at the Resurrection Parish, a few miles away from Santa Isabel, as well as Peter and George who had been in seminary with me and who had left. We tried to walk the fine line between trusting our kids and giving the benefit of the doubt to the authorities. We often acted as a conduit between the residents and the city.

A community activist group known as the Brown Berets gained traction in the neighborhoods in the city, including those around Santa Isabel Church, which was in Boyle Heights. Their main platform was to take a stand against alleged police brutality. Some group members talked in radical ways. Some didn't. Protests and marches grew common. Some were organized by the Brown Berets. Some weren't. To show solidarity with the residents, Father Gabe and I often marched in the protests, chanting with others for change. As priests, we organized gatherings and opened dialogue of our own, sometimes at City Hall, sometimes at the cathedral. We always tried to keep things peaceful. City officials and the sheriff and his team began to listen to the residents more and make changes in their staffing and the way they treated residents and kids. But it wasn't all peaceful.

One day, Father Gabe and I heard there was going to be a march down Brooklyn Street, headed toward the sheriff station. It was slated as a peaceful demonstration, so we made plans to join it in hopes of showing solidarity and keeping it as diplomatic as possible. A crowd gathered, a few speeches were made, and the march began down the street. We brought a large bag of bread to give out in hopes of using it to keep the peace.

But things quickly turned ugly. Chants escalated. Fists clenched. Tension mounted. Police started lobbing tear gas canisters at the crowd. Father Gabe and I were right in the thick of things, coughing from deep in our lungs, our eyes blurry and stinging. We were dressed in our black suits with the white collars, clearly identified as priests, and we worked for some time to keep people calm and to help them disperse. Many of the marchers scattered immediately. But the rest of the crowd, the ones who stayed, were fed up, and the situation escalated no matter what we tried to do. Fights soon erupted. Shields and clubs came out. Police dogs were let loose. The street seemed to blow up in front of our eyes. In the end, we received the sad news after the scene was cleared that Rubén Salazar, a friendly reporter from the *Los Angeles Times*, had been killed when he was hit by a tear gas canister. It was a terrible day.

It felt confusing to be so close to life-and-death action like that. Love requires courage to wade in where people are drowning, I told myself, even if the river is swollen, the current fast racing.

I wish I could have stayed longer at Santa Isabel. In many ways it felt like the work of ministering to the residents was just beginning. But soon after the violent march I was transferred to another parish, south, to the city of Placentia in Orange County. The move wasn't due to the reporter's death. It was only because it was time for me to leave. Priests are typically moved by church officials every five years.

The pastor of the new parish immediately declared his suspicions of me. He'd heard about my involvement in the marches and was nervous I'd attract gang members and activity to his church. On my very first day in Placentia, the Hispanic community organized a march. Sure enough, a crowd ended up in our church parking lot with a bullhorn, shouting that the city and the church were neglecting that part of the town. The pastor accused me of starting the demonstration, but I reassured him it was all a coincidence. I helped him address some of their concerns.

In spite of the march, Placentia proved a calmer environment overall. Soon the church held a parish picnic, and about two hundred families came. The associate pastor, Father Dennis, took me under his wing and offered to introduce me around to all the church members. The thought of meeting stranger after stranger made my hands clammy and my throat dry, but Father Dennis insisted and led the way. He'd only been at the parish about six months, but already he'd memorized the names and addresses of all the congregants, including their children. Everybody seemed to like him a lot, and they appreciated his courtesy of learning who they were. I did okay at the picnic, and Father Dennis's example made a real impression on me. I saw how that type of caring for people, just learning their names, can be a further marker of love, and I made a mental note to immerse myself in the lives of community members as quickly as I could.

The people who'd protested in the church parking lot had made many good points, I thought, and as I got to know some of them, I tried to help wherever I could. We started a Spanish-speaking Mass and some smaller prayer and growth groups comprising Hispanics, as well as a strategically mixed youth group. The parish was able to hire a full-time youth minister, Dave Wolf, who had a connection with a camp over on Catalina Island, and he and I soon led a weeklong retreat there. About half of the kids we worked with had never been in a boat. Some hadn't even seen the ocean, although they lived only about forty minutes away.

✤ ✤ ✤

I'd come to this new assignment thinking that life in Orange County would be easier than it was in East L.A., but I quickly realized life holds forth difficulties for everybody, no matter the color of his skin or his socioeconomic situation. One thing I absolutely needed to do so I could continue to help people was to overcome my shyness and fear of people. I'd seen some success in ministry already, but this one albatross of personality continued to weigh heavy around my neck, as it had for years. Whether I was in the middle of a march or meeting groups of new congregants, the temptation to panic always existed.

I remembered back to 1960 when I was eighteen and in the Sea Scouts, the oceangoing branch of the Boy Scouts. We refurbished an old forty-foot U.S. Navy surplus launch, fixed its diesel engine, and put a sail on it, too. One of our first tasks was to escort a girls' choir to Naples in Long Beach to do some Christmas caroling. My father was in charge of the cruise, and I manned the engine compartment. Everything went well until we hit a submerged sandbar and the engine housing collapsed on me, cutting my hand. Dad yelled to me to put the engine in reverse, but I panicked and yelled that I could not do it. I was afraid to make a mistake. Fortunately, my cousin Fred jumped to my aid and put the engine in reverse for me. In a quieter moment later, I saw how my panic had placed everyone aboard in danger. I resolved that I would never again let my feelings of panic endanger others.

That was easier said than done. The fix was a gradual process over the years, one that Shayla had had a big hand in. But I understood that in some ways, I was responsible for making this change with God's help. I realized that the courage to love others wouldn't become part of my life automatically, and bravery wouldn't simply show up one day and take over my life. The quality of fearlessness would emerge only when I chose it. I'd still be placed in frightening situations, but I would need to press forward anyway. That proved to be God's invitation to me on lots of occasions in ministry.

One evening about 10:00 p.m. while I was at the Placentia parish house, I received a phone call. The woman on the other end was frantic, saying her husband was in their house with a loaded gun and making threats. She didn't know if he was going to shoot himself or her or someone else. I told her to hang up and call the police, but she immediately declined, saying that if the police arrived, then her husband would get really upset and someone was bound to get killed for sure. She asked me—begged me—to come over and talk with him. Only a priest would do, she insisted.

I did not want to talk to a crazy man with a gun. Priest or no priest, my love for others had its limits. Putting my life on the line wasn't something I'd signed up for. Yet, while I was still on the phone with the woman, a memory flashed through my mind.

When I was nineteen, the year after the Sea Scouts debacle, we were returning from Catalina on our ship. It was called the *Alamitos*, named after a little city in Orange County, and this time we were sailing with a strong wind back toward Long Beach where we had our dock. I was acting as quartermaster for the voyage for the first time and responsible for ensuring that certain drills and procedures were followed. One by one, I ticked the drills off. We held a fire drill. A first aid drill. A compass drill. A knot tying drill. There was one I was forgetting. *What was it?* I wondered. *Oh yeah, the man overboard drill.*

Without thinking any further, I jumped out of the boat. The crew members were all responsible Scouts, and I expected the proper procedure to be followed immediately like it had been done for all the other drills I'd run. But there was a big problem.

No one saw me jump.

We were right in the middle of the strait—thirteen miles away from Catalina and thirteen miles away from Long Beach. The sea was choppy, and there was no way I could swim to shore. I'd failed to put on a life jacket too—a huge mistake. I was a good swimmer and could tread water for an hour or more, but what would happen after that? From the midst of the sea, I watched our ship sail off into the distance. I couldn't call out; nobody onboard would hear me. Even the tall mast of the sail soon disappeared.

I scanned the horizon. There were no boats, no signs of life. Nothing. There was no land to be seen anywhere, as far out to sea as we were. The salt water slapped my face. How could I be so stupid? I was wearing only a swim-suit, no shirt, no hat against the sun. If I didn't drown, then my head would burn to a crisp before long.

Only the waves surrounded me. My heart raced, and I wondered if this might be the end of my life. Was I in a right standing with God? Who would mourn me at my funeral? The temptation to panic was overwhelming. I'd lived nineteen years, and they were good ones, but I knew I didn't want my life to be over this soon. I had things I wanted to do, places I wanted to go, people I wanted to meet. I thought about all the pain my death would cause. My parents would be heartbroken, sure. My brothers and sisters too. My friends from school. I figured this was it.

Thank God, the crew proved to be great sailors and eventually noticed I was missing. In a scramble and with a prayer on their lips, they turned back and began to comb the area of water where they'd last seen me onboard.

This may have been a miracle. Someone spotted my head bobbing among the waves, a wet needle in a haystack of ocean. Just before the crew pulled me onboard, the fin of a shark appeared near my leg. My crew got me onboard just in time.

That memory made me say yes to the woman on the phone. God had protected me there in the water. God would protect me here with the man with the gun.

As I drove over to the couple's house in Placentia, my main thought was just to keep afloat, like I'd done in the ocean. If I didn't panic—and I hadn't, really, even while I was treading water for the thirty minutes it took for the ship to find me—then with God's help, I stood a chance of talking this man through whatever mental turbulence was troubling him.

The wife let me in through the front door. She was anxious and nearly in a panic herself. She told me her husband was still barricaded in the bedroom, still with his loaded gun. My knees knocked together, but I walked to the bedroom anyway, all the while whispering prayers under my breath, and softly rapped on the bedroom door, declared who I was, and asked if we could talk.

To my surprise, the man grunted out an "okay" and opened the door. He kept his gun level, pointing it away from me, but still keeping me within easy range. I asked him a few questions to start a conversation, just hoping to get him talking about something, anything. He opened his mouth . . . and a dam broke in his soul. He talked and talked and talked, pouring out all of his angst, all of his anxiety, all of his troubles.

I listened for a long time. As I prayed silently for a solution, the answer came. His problems were valid, but in many ways they were not as complicated as he'd first made them sound. After he'd talked them out, a clearer pathway was evident. He was very frustrated because after working hard all day, he would come home and his wife would have a list of jobs for him to do as soon as he walked through the door. He could not take it anymore. I told him that I would talk to his wife and work out a solution. I talked to her about welcoming him home, giving him a hug, letting him relax for a little while, bringing him a drink. Then she could ask him for the help she needed around the house. She agreed.

The last I heard, decades after that frightening incident, they're both still doing well, both still alive, both still living happily together.

⚜ ⚜ ⚜

On August 12, 1974, a child, who I loved, came into the world.

Shayla and Dave's first child, a daughter, was named Shayla Marie Ebner. Right away, they asked me if I'd be the godfather. I felt honored and said yes in an instant. I felt excited that they'd had a child. Their family was starting to grow. They asked me to baptize the baby too, and I agreed. I nicknamed her "Shaylita"—a Spanish-sounding version of the name meaning "little Shayla."

On the day of the big event, I held little Shaylita in my arms. She was red and scrunchy-faced, dressed all in white and cooing softly. I explained to the congregants how infant baptism, for a Catholic, is like welcoming a new person into a community of faith. The parents, grandparents, and godparents all formally take upon themselves the responsibility to see that the child will grow in grace and knowledge of God. I read a few passages from Scripture, then baptized the baby girl as a sign that Jesus died, was buried, and was resurrected to give us new life and a relationship with God. I dried the baby off and anointed her head with oil, a sign that she had a great purpose in her life—to minister as Jesus ministered, to care for others, to love others unconditionally from the heart. And then I lit a candle as a sign that she was called to be a light to the world. We prayed together, then had a big party afterward with a lot of food.

Three years later plus one day, another child was born to Dave and Shayla, a daughter, Davida. I loved her too, with all my heart. Again, I was called to baptize her. Again, it was a wonderful feeling for me to be included in Dave and Shayla's lives. Yes, of course, the thought flew across my mind as I held these precious little ones that I would never have my own children. But it was not a sad thought. The love I had for Shayla had been changing and growing to include Dave and now these little girls, changing and growing but not diminishing.

🌿 🌿 🌿

Much of my ministry would have been impossible if I'd had children of my own. My former classmate, Father Barney, invited me to use a month of vacation time to join him on a trip to Mexico. A family in the parish donated a well-worn mail van for the trip. We obtained a used projector, a generator, and movies in Spanish about the life of Christ, then hit the road.

We traveled down through Baja California and wound up in the mountains on a dirt road to a ranch where about three hundred people lived. For their livelihood, they raised and sold Brussels sprouts. We showed the movies, ministered to the people, baptized those who had not been baptized, and gave the children their First Holy Communion. All the people there were very poor, and for two weeks we slept in the van and ate only Brussels sprouts, tortillas, and beans. They had no electricity or running water.

From there, we drove miles through the desert to a small town on the coast, where they fished for lobsters. Again, we ministered to the people and showed the movies. For two weeks all we ate were lobsters and beans. I enjoyed going to the places that really needed ministry, but that van was a real stinkeroo by the time it was returned.

After five years of ministering in Orange County, it was time for me to be transferred again. I'd enjoyed the challenge of working with gangs back at Santa Isabel, so I asked the bishop if I could move back to East L.A. He moved me to Resurrection Parish in Boyle Heights where Father Gabe had been—a working class, mostly Latino neighborhood of about a hundred thousand residents.

This new assignment in love was a roller coaster right from the start. Again, the youths banded together immediately and said they didn't want a "gringo" for their priest. I bided my time, looking for an in with them.

Meanwhile, the parish pastor asked me to be in charge of seventeen different groups within the church. I tried, but I felt that a few of the groups didn't need a priest's direct involvement. A few others comprised only elderly women who did nothing but sit around and gossip during their meetings. I just couldn't relate to them.

Instead, I went and talked to the kids and explained my vision for a youth group. They said they'd give me a tryout. I loaded up the church buses with church kids and gang kids alike and began to take them on retreats and outings—to the beach, the mountains, the movies—always with an eye to build relationships and increase their faith. I also had them participate in the Youth Encounter retreats that I had worked at with Shayla.

At first the parish pastor was angry with me. He thought I'd abandoned the groups he had put me in charge of and wrote me a long letter describing me as a failure and a disappointment.

I responded with what I hoped was tact and asked him to please be patient and wait. A number of months passed. I received a call from the local juvenile detention facility. They said, "What are you doing over there, anyway? Before you arrived, your area had more kids in juvenile hall than any other area in L.A. Now it doesn't have any."

I just chuckled. Love was working. The pastor wrote me another letter, this time apologizing. My experiments in caring for the community were paying off. The letter and the phone call were indications that I'd made the right choice. It felt validating on a ministry level, and it felt validating on a personal level too. I could see that it might have been difficult for me to work with these kids if I'd been married with children of my own. For instance, I might have felt a need to protect my own children from involvement with troubled youth. I realized again that God knew what He was doing in my calling.

Part of my ministry involved visiting patients in the hospital, and I ended up going to various hospitals in L.A. County several times a week. One day, a group of nurses had a big request for me. A man in one of the rooms was acting ornery. He'd yell and scream profanities at the nurses and generally act uncooperatively. Sometimes he even hit the nurses. They didn't want to restrain him, but that was the next step, one they hoped to avoid. Would I please talk to him?

In this instance again, I did not want to talk to this man. Offering this sort of love and empathy to combative people wasn't something I'd imagined when I became a priest, and these actions weren't anything I looked forward to doing. But I went into the room anyway and introduced myself, and the man called me every bad name in the book. I stood there until he paused to catch his breath, then I quickly interjected, "I only came in to greet you and wish you a good day." He picked up where he left off and continued to rage. I left.

The next time I came to the hospital I tried the same thing. Again, the man cursed nonstop until I left. Several weeks passed like this, and I continued to visit him regularly, simply putting up with the abuse.

About a month later, I came to the room, and the man growled, "Come in."

This change in behavior, minor as it was, frightened me at first I thought maybe this time he was lying in wait. He'd planted a gun and would blow my brains out when I got closer. But when I approached, the man said simply, "I want to confess my sins to God and start a new life."

I prayed with this man, once so hostile to the world. I prayed with him, and blessed him, and I invited him to discover a brand new life, regardless of the time he had left, thanks to the power and peace of Jesus Christ in his heart.

People often describe miracles in calculable terms. A dying man grows well again. An overzealous Sea Scout is found in the middle of the sea. I believe many miracles are less overt. They're harder to see, unless you know where to look for them.

When I left the hospital room that day, that same man, once so abusive, was quiet and breathing serenely, the first time I'd ever seen a composed look on his face. Not only that, but he said to me in sincerity, "Hope to see you soon." And the smallest hint of a smile tugged at one corner of his mouth.

🌿 🌿 🌿

Shayla and Dave had me over for dinner one night, I remember, in late 1979. When I ministered at Resurrection Parish, they didn't attend there, but we still found time to see each other every three to four weeks, just like always. Sometimes they'd have just me over. Sometimes they had me and a bunch of people over. Both ways were fine by me.

The girls were five and two years old then, and they frolicked happily in and out of the family room all the while, showing me their toys and sitting on my knee and singing me little songs and making me laugh. Shayla cooked a roast with potatoes and vegetables, and we all ate heartily, and talked and laughed and told stories, and it felt to me that nothing could be happier than this moment.

After dinner, Dave gave the girls baths, brushed their teeth, and put them to bed, while Shayla did the dishes and tidied up the kitchen. I sat in the kitchen and kept her company, and we talked lightly until Dave came down the stairs again. We went into the living room and relaxed in overstuffed chairs. Shayla went into the kitchen again and brought out coffee and cake, and for a while no one said anything of much substance. We were simply enjoying being together. At least that's how I felt.

When the cake was finished, our coffee cups empty, Shayla spoke first, this time asking me a deeper question. "How would you gauge the success of your ministry so far, Norm? Don't hold back. Let us know how it's truly going for you."

"It's going good," I said quickly. "Good—and difficult too. Some days are better than others." I told them about the man in the hospital who'd cursed me out for so long. How he'd become a different person. Shayla said it was encouraging to hear my ministry was going so well, and then she paused and looked at Dave.

"There's something we've been meaning to tell you, Norm," Dave said, but Shayla shook her head slightly, as if she wanted him to stop.

"Dave and I are going to be moving," Shayla said. She was always straightforward. "Up to Washington State."

I was stunned, instantly sad, thinking of the thousand miles that would now separate this family from me. All I could do was ask, "When?"

"It won't be for a few more months," Shayla said. "We've thought about this extensively. Prayed about it. We hate to leave behind all our friends here, but the girls are getting older now, and we don't want to raise them in Los Angeles. We want to give the children time and space, and we think that'll happen best in a more rural community."

Dave smiled. "We're going to move first to a rental just to get us set up there. Then we'll build our own home and move into that. It'll take about a year to build. We're looking at property on the East Fork Lewis River. It's beautiful, Norm, just beautiful. More trees than you could ever imagine. And the air is so clear."

"You're welcome to visit any time," Shayla added quickly. "In fact, we want to have you up as soon as possible."

Shayla poured us all more coffee then, and we sat up late talking more about their move. On the outside I tried to be happy for them, I truly did. The move would be great for the girls, and it made sense for the family. If I had kids of my own, I'm not positive that I'd want to raise them in some of the places I'd been in L.A. either.

Still, when I drove home that night, back to my room at the rectory, I needed to talk myself through this new situation. Dave and Shayla and the girls were all family to me now. One of my many families, as Shayla had predicted. But they were my closest family, other than my own parents, brothers, and sisters. In a perfect world, I guessed, distance would never separate us. We would all live close together forever.

As I pulled into the rectory's parking lot, I thought about now being thirty-seven years old. Forty was looming, and I didn't feel like a young man anymore. This was real life, all of it. Houses. Spouses. Children. Jobs. Career. Moving. Nothing stayed the same forever. Maybe not even love. Shayla had reassured me that I'd still be part of their family, but the distance between us all would be so great now. Instead of seeing them once a month, it might be more like once a year. Maybe twice a year, if I was lucky. I pictured all the important moments in their lives I was going to miss.

The answers lay beyond me, the coping mechanisms seemed beyond my grasp, and I didn't know what else to do. I brushed my teeth, changed into my pajamas, knelt by my bed to pray, and climbed under the covers. God's presence stayed with me as I drifted off to sleep. I did not find the answers to my specific questions that night, and when I awoke the next morning, I was still asking questions.

As I knelt by my bed again in preparation for a new day of ministry in Boyle Heights, I read from a passage of Scripture I didn't normally read devotionally—the love poem of Solomon, chapter eight. "Set me as a seal upon your heart, as a seal upon your arm; for love is strong as death, passion fierce as the grave. Its flashes are flashes of fire, a raging flame. Many waters cannot quench love, neither can floods drown it."

I felt a new resolve within me after reading that. God was leading us always, wasn't He? Love was strong, much stronger than I gave it credit for, and, somehow, everything was going to be all right.

CHAPTER 8

Facing Death

SHORTLY BEFORE SHAYLA AND DAVE and the kids moved away, I got to thinking that I wanted to move away too, although not out of Los Angeles. As a priest, days off were important to my life—as well as to the lives of my colleagues. The demands on us were constant, so time away was essential for our health. We were given one day off a week, a week after Christmas and Easter, and three weeks each summer. The days off were opportunities to get away from parish work and the stresses of living in the city.

On days off, with six of my friends in the priesthood—John, Roddy, Bill, Bob, Johnny, and Liam—I often went hiking. We packed a lunch, left in the morning, drove to the mountains and hiked until noon, ate lunch, hiked some more, then returned to L.A. and had dinner together. I found my head felt clearer out in the mountains, my vision renewed. In those days when a priest had his weekly day off, the rule was that he needed to be home before nightfall. After a while the rule was changed to allow for overnight stays, so we began dreaming of building a small getaway cabin located either at the beach or in the mountains.

A few of the guys weren't interested in the project, so that left just Bill, Roddy, and me. None of the three of us had any experience buying property. We pooled our savings and came up with $13,000, which seemed like a fortune, but we priced a couple of beach cottages and knew we weren't even close to a down payment. We started looking in the mountains.

For several weeks we looked and finally found a place on Pine Mountain that sat well in everybody's soul. There was no cabin yet, only a flat piece of land at the end of an undeveloped rural cul-de-sac. Yet the land itself was quiet. It was crowded in all the best ways with bushy stands of pine and oak trees and a stream running in front. At about six thousand feet elevation, it meant we'd see snow in winter; summers would be about twenty degrees cooler than L.A. It was only about an hour's drive from the city, close enough that we wouldn't be driving too long, and far enough away to feel like a change of scenery.

The asking price was $22,000. We didn't want to take out a bank loan—our salaries were about $300 per month each back then, and if we borrowed, it would take twice our lifetimes to repay. We found an agent and offered $13,000 for the lot, all we had. The broker just laughed. "No, really, that's as high as we can go," we said. He shrugged and took our offer to the seller.

To our surprise, the seller came back with a counteroffer of $20,500. We thought, *Wow, they're actually listening to us.* We offered our $13,000 again. They came back at $18,000. We thought, *Wow, they're still negotiating.* We offered our $13,000 again. They came back with $17,000. We'd saved up another $500 by then, so we offered $13,500 . . . and they accepted!

After the papers were signed, we each set aside $100 per month to save up for building supplies. I went to Dave and asked him to draw up some blueprints for us. He asked us what we envisioned, and we described a small place first, but he encouraged us to dream big—to imagine a place we could use not only for getaways for ourselves, but a place where we could bring groups for weekend retreats, too. Dave had a keen eye for design, and he sketched out plans for a large cabin with three sleeping areas, three bathrooms, a den, a meeting space, and a storage space. He wouldn't take a fee. I didn't know how we'd ever build anything that grand, but Dave was convinced it could be done.

Shayla thought the cabin was a great idea. She said it would do us real good. Dave and Shayla and the girls moved up north shortly after. I don't remember the actual saying of our good-byes. I think having the cabin project helped take my mind off any unrest I may have been feeling. Each time we friends saved up a bundle of money, we purchased supplies and headed up to the mountain to build. People from the parish helped us sometimes, but usually it was just us priests. We worked on it here and there, but steadily too. A year went by and another. All in all, it took us four years to finish it enough to live in. In the end, the cabin was better than we'd imagined. It became a real place of sanctuary, rest, and communion with God.

Before it was finished I went up to Washington to visit the Ebners. Dave had built the family house the first year they were there. It sat on twenty acres, and their property was everything he promised it would be. He showed me around, and we followed a deer trail right down to the East Fork Lewis River. Dave had designed the house personally, hired all the subcontractors, and did most of the work himself, laying every brick. Incredible views could be seen from every bedroom window. He built a horse barn too, thinking of the girls. In time, little Shaylita got a pony of her own, a Norwegian Fjord named Taffy. A few years later when Davida was old enough, she got one too.

The second year after they moved I visited them again. It was summertime, and we fished and hiked around their property and floated on inner tubes down the river all the way to a nearby park to cool off. Shayla had planted flowers everywhere. Roses, dahlias, daffodils. Outside their home, the grounds were a mass of color and beauty.

Shayla was driving her dream car by then, an older 1970 Lincoln Continental, one she'd inherited from relatives. It was white with a hint of blue on the body, and it had power windows, power seats, and power everything else. Shayla needed to take her driving test again when she moved to Washington, but she flunked it the first time. The instructor set up cones for the parallel parking test, but the Lincoln was humongous, too big to fit.

Dave and Shayla told me how they'd taken a cross-country trip in the Lincoln already and planned to take a few more. Those were the days before child seats, and the girls would take pillows and lie in the nook of the Lincoln's back window ledge as their parents drove. Shayla bought a newer Lincoln a few years later, a Town Car this time, almond in color. Dave got in an accident in it coming home from work one day. That Lincoln was totaled, so they bought another, this one cream colored. "That car saved your life," Shayla told him. "Of course we'll get another." I remembered how much a big, strong car meant to her.

When Shaylita turned seven, the family invited me up to perform her First Holy Communion. A few years later, I came up again to perform the ceremony for Davida's First Holy Communion. With each child, I talked to her beforehand to help her truly understand the meaning of what she was doing. Whenever we celebrate the Eucharist, we are reminded that we are called to love God, that Jesus died and rose again for us, that He gives himself to us in the Eucharist to help us on our journey. I was convinced the girls both understood what the Eucharist was all about, and it inspired me and humbled me to see the warm, childlike faith in their faces as each girl celebrated the ceremony. Being part of such watershed moments in the family's life underscored to me that I was special to them, if I'd been feeling at all doubtful.

A while later, Shayla returned to teaching, first at Our Lady of Lourdes in Vancouver, Washington, then a few miles north within the Battle Ground School District. She had her sights set on school administration. I knew she'd make an excellent principal. "It's all about the kids," she said to me again when she got the job.

Shayla's job progress acted as a marker of permanence in my mind. The Ebners seemed established in this new region of the country, settled in for the long haul in the Evergreen State. Although I wished I could see them more, my yearly trips had to be enough for now, and it felt all right. I had come to realize that time, marriage, child rearing, and even distance would not diminish my love for Shayla and this special family, nor theirs for me.

Our love was not ferocious, not a love of pining to be with each other every moment, but it was deep. And it was unstoppable. Nothing could stop our love. Not even death.

🌿 🌿 🌿

After five years of working in Boyle Heights, I was ready for a new challenge. In the years since I'd become a priest, I'd been disturbed by the numbers of college students I'd seen walk away from the faith. So I asked the cardinal archbishop if I could work as a campus pastor for two schools—East L.A. College and California State University, Los Angeles (CSULA). These were both commuter colleges then.

At first, the cardinal archbishop wanted me in a parish as usual, but when I described the intense need I saw and my drive to do this sort of ministering, he relented. The ministry would be fairly open ended at first. My task would be to show up on the campuses, develop relationships with students and staff, and then design ministry-oriented programs and implement them. The cardinal archbishop assigned me to a nearby parish—Saint Thomas Aquinas—in Monterey Park, which would pay my salary and act as a home base while I ministered on the campuses.

I remember well the first day of this new ministry. Before I left the rectory that morning I prayed, *Dear God, I don't know what I'm doing. I just know that You inspired me to do this, and the cardinal has allowed me to go in this direction. Please open all the doors I need to bring people closer to You. Amen.*

I drove a motorcycle in those days, a bigger Honda 750, so I rumbled my bike over to East L.A. College, parked it, walked up the front steps to the main building, and looked around. I didn't know where to go, who to talk to, or what to do. I needed God to move.

Right then, a security guard walked up, asked me who I was and why I was there. I wore a leather jacket for motorcycle riding, so I unzipped the jacket and showed him my clerical collar. I explained I'd been assigned to work with the students on campus.

"No, we don't have any priests," the guard said. "You're not supposed to be here. You should leave."

I repeated who I was and why I was there.

"Who's paying your salary?" the guard asked.

"The archdiocese, not the school," I said. "I'm here to help."

The man's frown changed to a smile, and he offered to introduce me around. I think he was worried at first that I wanted to proselytize on campus at the school's expense. But when he found out I was coming at someone else's expense to help students on their life journeys, he was satisfied with the arrangement. He took me straight to the president's office, where I introduced myself again. It turned out that the president was a Catholic. He'd been just as concerned about the students as I was and praying that help would arrive. The president ushered me straightaway to an empty office and told me it was mine. He secured secretarial help for me and had his staff get me a phone and a campus phone number. With the president's stamp of approval, everyone I met said, "Welcome. Welcome. We're glad you're here." I silently breathed a prayer of thanks. In less than one day, doors had opened for me at the first school. I had everything I needed to get to work.

The next day I prayed the same prayer—that God would open all the doors I needed—and headed over to the other campus at CSULA. Same as before: Right away I ran into a man who asked who I was and what I was doing. I explained, and he exclaimed, "My gosh, do we ever need you around here!" He was one of the vice presidents and he walked me over to the president's office to introduce me. Same as yesterday, immediately I was provided with an office, phone, and secretarial help. I was amazed that God opened doors yet again.

But it wasn't all smooth.

One of the other vice presidents at CSULA called me into her office shortly and informed me that she, for one, did not want me here—and she carried lots of influence around the school. I mentioned that I already had the president's approval, but she waved her hand in dismissal and insisted that I leave. As I walked out of her office I spotted an article from *Time* magazine on her bulletin board. The headline read, "We train youth how to make a living, but not how to live." I turned on my heel, pointed to the article, and said, "Look—that's the reason I've come." She still wasn't impressed and told me to beat it.

But I didn't. I left her office but I hung around, praying that God would open the door fully.

A few days later, a luncheon was held for all the faculty and staff. Somehow, I was invited and ended up sitting near the hostile vice president. Everything seemed smooth until I noticed her turning white and clutching at her throat. No one seemed to notice except me. I turned to her and asked if she wanted me to do the Heimlich maneuver. Frantically, she nodded. Sure enough, a tiny piece of meat had lodged its way in her throat. I did the Heimlich, and out it popped.

After that we were the best of friends. I guess she figured a priest could be of some use after all. I had to smile to myself at the way God sometimes chooses to work.

The campus ministries soon gained traction. The diocese sent a nun to help, and we set up a variety of programs and secured buildings to use as meeting centers. We set up workshops on effective relationships, self-esteem, personality types, and faith. We counseled students looking for direction, which seemed to be about everyone we met. A number of students described how three professors in particular consistently knocked God, so I gathered a few other ministers and a rabbi and we set up a friendly debate between the professors and us on the existence of God. We held Masses and worship services at the student centers.

Students responded favorably. Our workshops and services were packed from the get-go. Our debate was a raging success. Students always wanted counseling. The Masses and worship services were passionate and well attended. We set up retreats for the students that helped them navigate difficult times with their families, life choices, and relationships. The seminary noticed the burgeoning campus ministries and sent out an additional three seminarians to talk with students and help out wherever they could. My dream was becoming a reality, and I loved the new ministry where God had called me.

But there were dark days ahead. One morning in 1983 while at CSULA, an announcement came for people to take cover because a young man was brandishing a gun on campus. I received a call for help and ran toward the location of the man, praying as I ran. Guards ran toward the man too. So did policemen.

By the time I got there, the young man was lying in a pool of blood from a gunshot wound to the chest. He was still breathing, murmuring in pain. I crouched by his head and, using a cue from Shayla's many examples of direct communication with me, jumped straight to the point.

"You are going to die soon," I said to the young man. "It's time to make your peace with God."

He looked straight at me and answered, "I want to do that. I'm sorry. Will God forgive me?"

I assured him that Christ had forgiven the thief who hung on the cross next to Him, and that the thief was in paradise today because of that grace. The man prayed with me. His countenance changed from agony to peace.

And then he died in my arms.

🌱 🌱 🌱

In the mid-1980s, Father Tom Hedberg, the director of the Youth Encounter retreats, expanded the programs, and the demand for them spread like wild-fire. Since I'd been a principal leader at the retreats for years, I was asked to help lead events in Boston, Salt Lake City, Hawaii, and South Africa. Shayla wasn't able to volunteer at the retreats then due to her responsibilities at home and work, but I was still free to travel extensively.

I went to the island of Maui for several years in a row and got to know literally most of the residents and youth who lived there. Later, as my nieces and nephews graduated from high school, I took them to this retreat as grad-uation presents. More than once, they'd comment, "Wow, you know every-body here!"

In 1985, I ministered in South Africa for a month. It was during the height of apartheid, and I received my introduction to the horrible mandated racial segregation when I needed to use the restroom at a mall in Johannesburg. I went into the one I thought was marked "men," but people yelled at and chastised me, accusing me of trying to start trouble. Only then did I realize I'd walked in the restroom for black men only. I was lucky I was only repri-manded. I could have been arrested.

I wanted to know more, so contacts snuck me into Soweto, the large, blighted section of Johannesburg where blacks were ordered to live. Whites weren't allowed. The differences in infrastructure and accommodations were jarring. Homes in Johannesburg looked comfortable, with indoor plumbing and paved streets outside. Homes in Soweto looked nowhere near as nice, with unpaved streets and outdoor plumbing only.

The people I met in Soweto invited me to give a talk. I spoke on the nature of improbability, and used as an illustration the bumblebee, who in theory should not be able to fly but can anyway. I encouraged them to believe that one day apartheid would end, even though it seemed so improbable at the moment. To say thank you, they sang for me a cappella—a hymn of hope in beautiful six-part harmony. I cried.

One of our goals in establishing Youth Encounter in South Africa was to help break apart apartheid. We held five retreats while I was there, and we purposely invited to each fifty Caucasians, fifty blacks, fifty people of mixed race, and fifty continental Indians. Each retreat started the same, with each ethnic group sticking to itself. To counteract this, we formed mixed-race teams for discussion groups and socializing.

As each retreat progressed, it was amazing to see the ethnicities blend together. At first, people would be afraid to talk to each other. Then they'd begin to talk and open up. Soon, they'd realize they weren't so different from each other after all. Friendships formed. At the end of each retreat, the new relationships were beautiful, and many tears flowed as people let go of long-standing prejudices and hatred, finding new love for one another.

Somehow, word got out to the police about what we were doing in Johannesburg, and they raided our retreat center at night while I was there. Everyone was scared. We thought we'd all end up in jail, and I started praying that God would close the eyes of the authorities so love could continue.

The center was an old sprawling compound of a church that had been pieced together over the years with one building tacked onto another. If a person didn't know his way around, then the buildings could be a maze. Sure enough, the police searched room to room, but for some strange reason that night they could only find the white people. After a while, the police shrugged and left.

After we returned to the United States, the retreats continued in South Africa, and eventually more than one hundred thousand people attended them. The retreats helped launch a movement and it spread to six other African countries, including the island nation of Mauritius, a country that was radically changed for the better in subsequent years due in great part to the reconciling ministries of the retreats.

Years later I flew back to South Africa for the twenty-fifth anniversary of the retreats. One man came up to me and said, "You literally saved my life. My life was down in the dumps and I didn't know where to go. You brought these retreats and showed me the love of God. I found hope again."

I found out then how many of the students and young adults I'd worked with in South Africa had continued to be involved in social protests and demonstrations. A few of them died in the protests, while others became victorious, eventually playing key roles in helping to end apartheid. I thought, *Jiminy Christmas, I was part of history here. Something horrible ended, and more love was brought to a country where real change occurred.*

One of the most powerful signs of the power of God's love was found in the tiny island nation of Mauritius, just off the coast of the African continent, which we also visited again. In the years that had passed, the country had become widely known for the love people there have for each other. Unemployment and crime were low because of the national harmony. In spite of many different races and religions present on the island, there was little discord or strife. When I saw that, I thought, *Love really does change things. I've always known it. Here is one more one more example that proves this.*

❧ ❧ ❧

The darkest days for me personally began when I came home from South Africa. I still had a bit of vacation time left, so I headed up to Washington to see Shayla, Dave, and the kids. That was the first time I'd ever driven my motorcycle that far north, and I rode along the coast for a long way, stopping to see a friend in Sacramento and another in Oakland. I saw another friend there who had an extra car, and he warned me strongly about continuing my ride up to Washington. "Please use my extra car," he said. "I beg of you, Norm. Something bad will happen. I can feel it."

I thanked him, but said no. I was an experienced rider and loved riding my bike. The summer air was clear and warm. I rode up to Battle Ground without a hitch and spent a good few days with Dave and Shayla and the kids.

On the morning I was set to leave, the kids hugged me tight, Dave shook my hand good-bye, and Shayla embraced me and looked straight into my eyes. She wore a strange look of concern, one I hadn't seen in years.

"You be careful," she said and stared at me a long minute. I was going to ask her if something was wrong when her brow unfurrowed and she quickly grinned. She gave me a playful thump on the side of my helmet and added, "Make sure you always wear your brain bucket—okay?"

I grinned and nodded, started my bike's engine, waved, and took off down the road. My first destination was my sister Doris's house in Willow Creek in northern California, and I hoped to make the trip in one day, even though I wasn't moving too fast. I meandered across the Columbia River and out through Portland to the Oregon Coast. There, I hit Highway 101 and turned south, breathing in the fresh salt air, marveling at the trees and hills and water.

Ahead of me was a milk truck.

I remember that well because it had words on the back. The truck was large, and it had square sides. We were both doing about sixty miles per hour on the winding two-lane highway.

The trucker put on his blinker to turn left and started to make his turn.

I thought, *No problem, I'll just pass him by on the right.*

But in an instant the truck stopped. My bike had nowhere to go. Simultaneously, I stomped on the foot pedal that activates the back brake and clutched tight the hand lever that activates the front brake. The back of the milk truck grew large in my vision. My motorcycle was still doing at least fifty.

After that, I remembered nothing.

CHAPTER 9

Light Streamed through the Window

VOICES AND SHOUTS AND CONFUSION came at me from all around. Someone kept asking over and over, "Is he dead? Is he dead? Is he dead?" I knew I'd been in a crash, but I didn't know how bad it was. I knew I was lying on the ground in the dirt, because above me I could see the clear blue Oregon sky. I knew my motorcycle was nowhere near me, and I knew nothing felt right in my body. That's about all I could discern.

I could smell blood, so I tried to feel around to check the extent of my injuries, but it hurt too much to move. Blood seemed to be oozing from everywhere. My legs. My chest. My left arm. My fingers. My right leg looked like a piece of chalk that had been stepped on. My left leg, right above the ankle, was lying at such an angle that it looked to be nearly severed. Through holes in my jeans I could see it was still holding on by a few pieces of skin.

Death felt imminent. I could sense it lurking right around the corner. I asked myself if I was ready to go. *Dear God,* I prayed, *I guess I'm going home to You today. I feel ready. Prepared. Please welcome me home.* I wasn't afraid to die, only wistful, like something important wasn't finished yet.

I wished for ice. I don't know where that thought came from. Maybe it was a prayer.

Someone knelt over me. Her voice sounded calm, reassuring, "I was in the car a few lengths behind you," the voice said. "I'm a nurse. I just bought some ice at the store. Hold on—I'm going to pack you in it."

I tried to speak. Tried to thank her as she worked. Maybe she was an angel. No, she was a person. I tried to focus my eyes on her face.

Someone else knelt over me. The face was unsmiling. Concerned. Bearded. "I just radioed the hospital," the stranger said. "They're only three miles away. Hang on—help will be here soon."

Again I tried to speak. No words came. I felt confused. Jumbled. I prayed some more. This time I just tried to be silent and listen to God. I don't know what I expected. A bright light maybe. A hand outstretched that welcomed me home. God was speaking to me in the silence, I sensed that much. But He wasn't saying, "Come on," waving me home like I expected he would. He was saying simply, "Be still. Know that I am God. I am here."

The ambulance arrived, and the medics started working on me. I decided that if I was dying, then I would die happy. When I found my voice, I started joking with people. I told them I was upset because my pants were ripped. Voices mixed together above me, and I stopped talking. My mind drifted to the people I knew and loved. My parents. My siblings and their families. Danny and my friends from school. The people in all the ministries I'd been a part of.

Shayla.

I blacked out then, I think, and sort of wavered in and out from then on, because I don't remember the ambulance ride. I knew I arrived in the hospital. I knew a flurry of white-gowned doctors and medical personnel were working on me. I knew I was lying on a hospital gurney with a crosshatch of tubes running in and out.

The priest stationed at the hospital came to see me. My eyes fluttered open, then shut, then open again just a hair. Any priest worth his salt has seen his share of vehicle accidents, especially a priest who ministers near a busy winding road as this man did. But this one walked into the emergency room, took one look at the mangled mess that was me, and immediately threw up in the garbage can. My eyes closed, then opened again slightly. The priest composed himself, wiped his mouth and got a drink of water from the sink, then came near my gurney. He administered anointing and the blessing for the dying, and

I realized he was performing last rites on me. He was preparing a dying person's soul for death. My eyes closed again. *Even the priest believes I'm going to die.*

When I opened my eyes again, a surgeon was standing over me. "Father Norm? Can you hear me?" His voice was clear and loud. "I need to amputate your leg. But I know a preacher needs his feet, so I'm going to sew your leg back on because there's a slim chance it will take. I don't want to give you any false hope. Your leg injury alone is quite bad. There's a lot of dirt and gravel in the wound that we can't clean out. The only way your leg will be saved is by a miracle."

My eyes closed then. I don't know how long I was out.

When I awoke, there was a small carton of milk in front of me with a straw. I wondered if it was from the milk truck I'd hit.

The next day I was awake when my mother walked into the room. It was a different room, not the emergency ward, and I gathered she'd flown up as soon as she'd heard about the accident. As a nurse, she'd seen everything. She looked right at me, then walked straight out again.

"Mom," I called out. My voice sounded weak, far away, soft. I wanted her near.

A few minutes later she came back into the room and asked, "Norm—that's not you, is it?"

I gurgled the affirmative.

"I didn't recognize you at first," Mom added. "You look like a frog."

Those were her exact words. Out of her love for me, she was trying to be kind, trying to lighten a grave situation with a joke. I was so happy to see her. So relieved. She got right to work as only a mother can do. I drifted in and out. When I came to again, Mom was still by my side.

When my mind began to clear, one of the first things I wanted to know was the extent of my injuries. Both my legs and both arms were up in traction—I could see that much—and my face felt all swollen. That's where the frog comment had come from. Mom took a deep breath and began the explanation...

In all, seventeen of my bones had been broken badly, so much so that I was missing entire parts of the bones in places. The bones were either pulverized or had vanished—broken pieces were knocked out of my body by the impact of the crash.

My left leg, right above the ankle, was severed except for a few pieces of skin. Lots of flesh and bone had been lost in that area. The leg had been sewn back on, and the doctor had knit the ends of the bone together using a piece of steel and seven screws to hold it in place. It was the leg that only a miracle could save. Thick layers of gauze and casting were wrapped around the lower part of that leg, and the dressings looked eerily brown and blood soaked.

My right leg was broken at the thigh. Four inches of bone were crushed completely. Doctors put a piece of steel in that thigh too, with another seven screws to hold it in place.

Almost all of my ribs were broken.

My left arm was broken. They put a piece of steel in there too, along with another seven screws. My right arm was messed up. Severely cut and scraped. Several fingers were broken.

Fortunately, my head and skull were still intact. My head was about the only part of me that felt untouched, except for the swelling. Also fortunate was the news of no internal injuries. This had surprised the whole the medical team. None of my broken ribs had pierced any organs, not even my lungs, which are located right behind the ribs.

As Mom described my injuries, I looked into her eyes. When she finished, I passed out. That was enough information for one day. When I came to, Mom was still there. I passed out again and came to again. She was always there. My eyes opened and closed. Opened and closed. All the painkillers they were feeding me kept me foggy.

And then Shayla walked into the room.

It was morning, and she wore a simple pale yellow shirt with a collar with blue pedal pusher pants. She looked jaunty and fresh, and for a moment I imagined her on the front of a boat on the way to Catalina Island, the wind blowing through her hair. Then I snapped back to reality, and she was standing next to my hospital bed, her cool hand pressed against my forehead, her eyes growing moist with tears.

"Norm," she whispered. "I came as soon as I heard." And then she tried to smile, and it was a smile I knew was for my sake.

I was a mess.

Mom was out of the room then, I could see, and I lay flat on my back with various pillows propping up my arms and legs. I could smell my wounds. My face hadn't been shaved, and I was naked except for a rumpled sheet that covered my groin area. My legs and arms stuck out and up and were covered with tubes and bandages.

Laid before Shayla like this, in this moment of my darkness, I felt completely vulnerable, utterly without pretense. This was my body, broken and bleeding, and I wouldn't have held it against her if she turned away in disgust. If she threw up in a garbage can.

But Shayla did none of that.

"Can you see out the window, Norm?" she asked softly. "Just turn your head to the right a little. Good. That's it. See the sunlight shining through? It's streaming through your window, Norm. The sunlight. It's just streaming toward you."

It was so good to see her. So good.

Shayla sat like that beside me, without saying much more, for nearly an hour. She touched my forehead, my hair. She ran her fingers down the length of my face. In her fingers was the touch of warmth and life. I was completely at peace in her presence.

Then Shayla rolled up her sleeves and went to work. For several days she worked alongside my mother and the nurses, changing bandages, changing sheets, cleaning me, feeding me, praying with me, adjusting my arms and legs to new positions, unwrapping gifts and get-well cards and reading them to me, keeping track of medications and painkillers. All the while she radiated sunlight. She gave me cups of cool water. She existed as the tangible hands and feet of a ministering Christ. It was act after act of love.

My sister Doris and her husband Charlie came to the hospital and visited for a while. They drove across town and picked up my motorcycle from the wrecking yard. Surprisingly, the bike didn't look too bad, they reported. It had flown under the truck virtually unscathed.

The driver of the milk truck visited to pay his regards.

"I just wanted to see you and say hello," he said.

I tried to smile. Within me I held no anger against this man for stopping suddenly in front of me. Accidents happen.

"I can't quite believe this," he said, "but the bumper on the back of my truck is a quarter-inch-thick steel and has a huge bend in it now. Your bike didn't cause that bend. It was underneath my truck. Your body caused that bend."

Again I tried to smile. "Well, my body feels like I bent your bumper," I mumbled. It was a joke, and we both tried to grin.

My good friend Danny came and visited. He went out to the accident site and took some pictures and brought them back to show me. The blood was nearly cleaned up from the pavement. It looked like any old lonely stretch of highway again.

The guy who drove the tow truck came to visit me, along with his son. Both were complete strangers to me. They simply wanted to wish me well and let me know they were thinking about me, hoping all would be well soon. His son wanted to meet the crazy guy who'd kept joking while he was all smashed up.

All in all, I felt okay in my spirit, thanks to all the outpourings of kindness. I loved that my mom was there. I loved that Shayla was near me. I loved that so many people came to visit so quickly.

But I was worried too. I knew my leg wasn't healing as it should. I tried to imagine what life would be like with only one leg. How could I get around? How would I drive? Would I be in a wheelchair forever? How could I fulfill my calling with only one leg?

🌿 🌿 🌿

On Shayla's last day in the hospital, Mom was out of the room for a while, and Shayla sat with me for an hour without saying much. She needed to get back to her life, to her husband and family, to her job at the school, which was just about to start again for the new school year.

"I brought you a present," Shayla said at last. "I was going to give it to you before today, but somehow the timing didn't seem right."

"I didn't get you anything," I said.

She smiled while ignoring the comment and brought out a little gift bag, which she opened. Inside was a small wooden cross. "It's olive wood," she said. "It's meant to be a symbol." She stopped and held the cross a moment, looking at it curiously. I wanted to ask questions, but I could see something was churning within her. She cleared her throat and continued. "The cross represents sufferings, Norm, yet goodness can come through these sufferings, too. I want you to have this cross so you can remember the sacrifices we made in our personal lives of letting go of our relationship and not being married to each other. That was the gift we gave God. We let God use our lives the way he wanted to. We chose the pathway of obedience, and we can only believe that goodness has come because of that decision."

We didn't normally talk about that sacrifice or refer to "our relationship." I felt stunned for a moment; then I smiled as I realized the depth and significance of her gift. The cross was a sign that she really did care deeply about me, even now, even still. Nothing had diminished our love. It had grown and evolved, but it had not dampened. I felt appreciative, humbled, and blessed.

"Let me pray for you, Norm," Shayla added—and she didn't wait for me to answer. She touched me lightly on the forehead and closed her eyes. She thanked God that I didn't die. She thanked Him that I was being used by Him in ways of goodness. She prayed for my various injuries to heal. And she prayed specifically for my left leg—that a miracle would happen, and that I would keep the leg. Then she kissed me lightly on the cheek.

And then she was gone.

Later, when the doctor saw me on his rounds, he said, "You know, Norm, your left leg is showing some remarkable improvements today. If you would have asked me yesterday for the honest truth, I would have said there was no hope. But, today . . ." he paused and searched for words. "Just keep praying, that's all."

🌿 🌿 🌿

Days blended together in the hospital. Mostly my mind felt lucid, but I was in and out too. I had zero energy. I felt completely plowed. One day, a woman came into my room, having heard I was a priest. She sat at the foot of my bed and poured out her heart to me. I was in no shape to counsel anybody, and I fell asleep in the midst of her story. She wasn't happy with that, I found out later. She wanted advice, but I couldn't meet those sorts of expectations. All my energy was being used in trying to put my body back together.

Get-well cards streamed in from everywhere. Sometimes the count was up to two hundred cards per day. "Who are you, anyway?" a nurse asked one afternoon, her voice filled with incredulity. Shayla's phrase of long ago, "a father to many families," came to mind, but I said nothing.

Day after day, Mom stayed at the hospital and cared for me, and then it began to dawn on me what she had given up. When my accident happened,

Mom was only one month away from retirement and receiving her pension from work.

"Mom?" I asked one evening. "How come you're able to spend so much time with me? Won't they mind at work?"

She just smiled and said, "You're worth more to me than any of that."

Little by little, I pieced together the truth. By caring for me, Mom had lost her pension completely. Those were the contracted stipulations at the time. Her work did not grant her a leave of absence or a medical leave. She wasn't able to use vacation time. Mom had given up a lifetime of accumulated benefits for my sake.

All for the sake of love. There it was again—love beyond understanding that streamed like sunlight into my life.

🌿 🌿 🌿

I spent a month in the hospital in Oregon. They put me in a room that overlooked a beautiful park. I could look out the window, and I saw families on picnics. They played ball and chased each other around, and part of my decision to heal was so I could enjoy the outdoors again. After a while, they took me out of traction, which provided some relief. Both arms and both legs were still in casts.

One day I decided I'd try walking, so I asked the doctor to bring me a walker. He humored me and brought one over. I found I couldn't even move. The doctor just laughed, although not unkindly. "That's the spirit, Norm," he said. "Keep fighting to live."

A friend with a private pilot's license rented a small Cessna to take me home to Los Angeles. He loaded me and Mom onto the plane and took off, stopping only in Sacramento to refuel. The ride was pretty rough on me, but we made it.

Another friend met us at the airport, gave me a shot of something to mellow me out, and drove me over to Mom and Dad's house in Long Beach.

They'd put a hospital bed in their back bedroom, and Mom nursed me around the clock. An infection soon set in, as infections are prone to do, so they took me to St. Mary Medical Center in Long Beach, and I spent another month there. The doctor for infectious diseases did some tests. A couple of days later he came in with the news that it was a stubborn infection and only penicillin could stop it. I informed him I was allergic to penicillin. He went back for more testing. A couple of days later he returned, saying there was nothing to kill the infection, only something that would weaken it. He said we needed another miracle. I thought, by now, that I was running out of miracles, but once again, God had different ideas. The infection abated on its own within days, and I was able to say good-bye to the hospital and move back to my parents' house. Dad had a van, and he fixed up the back with a mattress and drove me to my doctor's appointments. Slowly, I began to heal.

I had a lot of visitors then. People came nearly every day to see me and wish me well.

My sister Phyllis, a physical therapist and a nun, got permission from her community to help in my rehabilitation. After lying in a bed for more than two months, I could barely move and my muscles were very weak. Phyllis worked with me for a couple of hours each day so I could get my muscle strength back. At the start, my mother came in and said, "Phyllis don't work him so hard." She could see that it hurt my already-pained body.

But Phyllis replied, "Norm has asked me to help him be able to walk again. The doctors told him it would be impossible because of his extensive injuries. Mom, if Norm really wants to walk, then he must work hard toward this goal." Mom left.

When my muscles were a bit stronger, Phyllis told me, "It's time now to see if you could get back into bed in case you fall out." Not knowing all that these words meant, I said, "Okay," and she pushed me out of bed. I didn't expect that and asked, "How am I going to get back in?" She said, "Figure it out" and left for a while. I learned.

When I was a little stronger and could advance to crutches, Phyllis asked me, "What would you do if you fell while using your crutches?" I knew her better by then and waited. Sure enough she pushed me and I fell to the ground. She simply waited until I could figure how to get up—and I did!

Soon I was back to work on crutches but feeling confident that soon I would be walking independently, thanks to Phyllis' loving me and caring for me during these rough recovery months.

I attribute my ability to walk today to Phyllis.

Oh, and I kept my leg— it never was amputated. It's the one where the toe is dislocated. When they sewed it back on, the doctor did not fix the toe because he did not think the leg would heal. Because of that toe, every step I take today is painful. Yet, that pain reminds me moment by moment that miracles do happen.

They truly do.

🌱 🌱 🌱

It took more than a year for me to recover fully from my motorcycle accident. Slowly I began ministering on the university campuses again. I'd walk around with crutches, talking with students, checking on the various programs. Little by little, all my limbs began to work normally again.

Another year passed. Toward the end of 1987, my dad started to feel sickly. His legs weren't working well by then, and some days he used a wheelchair. He'd sold his shop and was having a hard time adjusting to not working. It was a big change for a man who'd worked hard all his life, who'd found so much of his identity in working.

On January 1, 1988, my cousins threw a New Year's Day party. Dad went to the party and had one bright experience of joy. He talked easily to many relatives and old friends he knew. He enjoyed the food and music. He really had a ball.

The next morning when Mom woke up, Dad's body was lying next to her in bed. But it was only his body, not his spirit. God's hand had reached down one more time, this time to beckon Dad home.

When a man's father dies, it sets that man back a ways. That's how I felt. I knew my father was with the Lord in glory, but even so, I was sorry to see Dad pass. I missed him every day, and I still miss him all these years later.

All throughout that year—1988—it felt as if a black cloud hung over me. The campus ministry was still going steadily but had reached a plateau. I'd been there eight years, longer than any ministry I'd been a part of. God was telling me to move, but I kept resisting him, telling him no, I did not want to leave. I loved that campus ministry and didn't want to let go.

I should have known better than to resist God.

That year, one by one, each component of the ministry began to crumble. Staff left. Programs died out. Then, most hurtful of all, I was accused of taking inappropriate actions with female students. What happened was that a troubled student grew angry with me because of the chaos in his life and his unmet expectations of how I would help him through it. In his anger, he snuck into my office and went through my file of contacts, telephoning person after person, spreading lies about me. The accusations were totally baseless, and soon were proven so, but the episode left me feeling worn through.

Finally, I obeyed God and quit the campus ministry. I needed a break. My own accident, my father's death, the last season of difficult ministry—all the pressure had accumulated and I felt out of gas, exhausted, burned out. I didn't know where to turn except to God, the One I'd been resisting. The One who could give me new life.

"Come away and rest a while," I read in the Gospel of Mark, the words of Jesus to His disciples. I was granted a sabbatical, so I took those words to heart. During the next few months, I walked. I read. I prayed. I talked to friends. I immersed myself in Scripture. I did little else, and slowly the spark for life began to return.

It's funny, when I was feeling so down, I began to meet other people who struggled with the same sorts of things. Depression. Feelings of neglect. Sorrow. Grief. Addictions. When people found out I was personally struggling with burnout, they opened up to me even more. People at lunch counters. People I met in stores. People at retreats I went to. Old friends who phoned to say hello and see how I was doing. It wasn't just Catholics either. People from all beliefs and world views expressed how life had a nasty habit of punching hard. How they needed hope and healing.

Along the way, I met some priests who'd been accused of inappropriate actions, and these men, sadly, had been correctly accused. That was intensely troubling, and I took this dishonor personally as a marker of shame upon my profession, because I've always loved children with the correct sort of love —a love that guides and nurtures —and I would never do anything to harm anyone, much less a child. I could not go along with the notion that some people put out there, that the molesters were monsters- -they were still human beings. But they were definitely messed up. That much was for sure.

As a whole, the Church authorities began to formally recognize some of these troubles right around that time, and the issue of molestation in particular bears close scrutiny, even now. Rules began to change in the Church. Offices were fitted with more windows. More checks and balances were put into place. No longer could a priest drive a student anywhere if it was just the two of them alone in the car. The Church took some definite hits, and some of those hits were correctly attributed.

But others weren't. What upset me greatly was the overall culture of suspicion that grew during that season. A few bad apples had created this climate for everyone else. One day, I walked into a restaurant and a woman yelled at me, "Hey, there's a priest. Do you molest kids?" Everyone in the restaurant turned and stared. I wanted to shout, "No—do you?" But I just shook my head and sat down for lunch.

Throughout the years of ministry, I've heard literally thousands of formal confessions, and I know that molestations happen with alarming frequency. Yet strangely, it's not just single men who perpetrate this horrible action. I hear from coaches and youth leaders, most of them married. I hear from parents. Relatives of the abused. Stepfathers. Uncles. Grandparents. Some grandmothers even. Whenever molestations are reported in a confessional, I try to convince the person to report it. Confessions are deemed sacred and are completely confidential, so these are very tricky situations, as I am forbidden to report a crime myself. I am always relieved when a person listens to my advice and makes a report.

Fortunately, I believe the winds are changing, and in good ways. In my first decades of being a priest, children used to run up to me at church and hug me. But then when all the headlines about priests molesting children started to come out, a culture of uncertainty was created, and parents would pull their kids away from church leaders. It's not like that anymore. Now, in my fifth decade of formal ministry, kids at church hug me again. And that's a good thing—for children to know and love their religious leaders.

But I'm getting ahead of myself here.

When my sabbatical was through, I was assigned to a new parish, this time in Fillmore, California, about half an hour north of Los Angeles. It was where I found God working through me in even more powerful ways than ever before.

For a while it would be a good, long season of upswing. Yet, the dark days weren't completely behind me. Looming far off on the horizon was something I never could have imagined. A large storm was coming that would rock my world forever.

CHAPTER 10

How the Years Slip By

WHEN I DROVE UP THE FREEWAYS north and northwest to Fillmore, California, for the first time, I marveled at how close I was to the City of Angels, and yet how far away I felt from the big city hustle and bustle in this new destination. The sky grew misty as I headed over the line into Ventura County. The ocean with its salty coolness was maybe twenty miles away, and I smelled the fragrant tang of orange groves in the air, the rich, pungent loam of the hills surrounding the town.

I parked my car in front of the Saint Francis of Assisi Church, my new parish. Next door was a small manufactured home that would serve as a rectory, my living quarters. By the time I'd reached the church, the hot afternoon wind had risen and blown the cooler mist away. The sky had become overcast and glary, and I needed to squint. The road to Fillmore might have offered a homespun and comforting feel, but I knew that any town, large or small, held out its offerings of problems too, and I wondered what I would find here.

I met the pastor, Monsignor O'Byrne, and he showed me around. I was surprised to find out that he didn't speak any Spanish. There were three big migrant camps in the area, he explained, with about two hundred workers each plus their families, yet nobody was reaching out to them. They mostly picked oranges and other crops. Historically, tension had existed between the whites and Hispanics in that area, and some people looked down on the migrants as second-class people. But I knew they were God's children, same as everybody else, so I thanked the pastor for the information and went right to work.

Over the next few weeks and months, I drove out to the migrant camps many times and met the workers and set up some services for them in addition to inviting them back to our church. We soon started a Spanish Mass at our church, which the Hispanic community said they appreciated. The other pastor was Irish and he cracked a lot of Irish jokes, which pretty much fell on deaf ears, they told me, because they just didn't understand the references. But pretty soon the attendance at church doubled, and we built up a strong, interracial community of faith, both in Fillmore and at our smaller mission church in the town of Piru near the lake. Soon, the people of another small town, Val Verde, asked me to help establish a church there. We were able to rent a community building in the park on Sundays and hold a service there.

About a year and a half after I came to Fillmore, the pastor retired and the diocese asked me to take over entirely. By then the ministry involved leading all three of the churches—the one in Fillmore, a town of about fifteen thousand people; the one in the nearby town of Piru, population two thousand; and the one in Val Verde, population about a thousand. I said yes, and for the first bit of time, I had a rough go of it simply because of the workload. The diocese had promoted me, but they hadn't found anyone to fill the associate position that had previously been my job. Among the three churches, I held eight Masses per weekend, both in English and Spanish. Service times were staggered, so that meant I'd do one Mass at Fillmore, then drive over to Piru and do another, then drive to Val Verde and hold one, then back to Fillmore and hold one there, and so on, and so on. For several months I racked up a lot of miles on my car, and during that season I felt quite alone. After a while, the diocese hired both an associate and a youth pastor, so that was helpful. Then Sister Guadalupe, a nun, came to help in the ministry too, and it felt like more of a team effort after that.

The previous pastor had started a building project at the church in Fillmore, but it had only just begun when I arrived. It was my job to finish it.

Plans called for an educational building with four classrooms and a new office building. Given my background at the metal shop, I felt comfortable around blueprints and general contractors, and I kept a careful watch on details. "Change orders" are a normal part of any construction project, where plans need to be altered midstream. But during the entire building project, we only experienced one change order, thanks in part to my watchful eye, which I felt good about when it was all completed. I wished every part of ministry at the church went that smoothly.

In the early morning hours of January 17, 1994, I was asleep when my room started shaking violently. I was up in a flash, groggy though my heart was racing, mindful enough to realize a massive earthquake was rocking the foundations of the land. The shaking stopped in ten seconds. All went eerily quiet. I knew the repercussions of anything that massive would be large. Right then, Jim Higgins, who was helping in the ministry, banged on my front door.

"The sky's on fire," he yelled. "Downtown's all messed up."

I ran to the phone to call 911, but phone lines were down. Jim and I hurried downtown. A gas line had ruptured near a mobile home park. Huge flames shot thirty to forty feet into the air. Two walls of a nearby apartment building had slid away. The building was still intact, and we could see people inside, stumbling around in their pajamas. Everywhere we looked, cars were flattened and rubble had fallen into the street. Pretty much the entire downtown was destroyed. "The highway into town is wrecked!" someone shouted. "No one can reach us."

It was true. We were all alone.

I'd learned from prior life instances of crisis that I couldn't allow myself to panic. That learned response kicked in now. Sister Guadalupe joined us, along with Vidal, our youth pastor, and we started making plans. Firemen and volunteer rescue workers from the town were already going building to building, so we knew that people would quickly need shelter, food, and clothing. I gathered the various church leaders in the area and went to work.

Hours slid into hours, and days slid into more days. Sleep eluded us. Little by little, news trickled in via battery-powered transistor radios. Those were the days before cell phones and the Internet. President Clinton declared the San Fernando Valley a disaster area, but surprisingly not the town of Fillmore. We learned later that nobody from the outside had heard any reports of damage from us. The quake had measured 6.7 on the Richter scale, and the damage all over the region was massive. Richard Riordan, the mayor of Los Angeles, declared a state of emergency. All flights in and out of LAX were canceled. All schools were closed. Power was out everywhere. Phone service was down. Breaks in a number of water and gas lines were reported. The scoreboard at Anaheim Stadium had fallen, crushing the upper deck seating. Thousands of other buildings throughout L.A. were damaged. Sections of Interstates 5, 14, and 10—all major thoroughfares— were severely damaged. Throughout the region, some fifty-seven people were reported dead.

Since our facility in Fillmore was the largest church property in the area, we turned it into a huge relief center. We got hold of any groups we could, however we could, and help poured in from FEMA, the Red Cross, the Salvation Army, World Vision, the Small Business Association, the Mennonites, the Baptists, the Catholic charities, and various other agencies. Workers showed up from all over the country, wondering where to go and what to do. We helped organize them into groups and sent them this way and that to help repair houses and roads. We set up soup kitchens and food banks, tents where gently used clothing was offered, counseling services, and repair services.

Little by little, order returned from chaos. Services were restored. Homes and businesses were rebuilt. Life gradually returned to normal, brick by brick, nail by nail. When I look back on it now, I realize it was an amazing time to be ministering at Fillmore, to be there and be able to pour out energy when people's needs were so desperate, to be able to bring together the community in many ways and help people rebuild their lives. I feel honored and privileged to have been part of their history.

✤ ✤ ✤

I mentioned a storm was coming, one that would rock my world forever. As devastating as it was, the earthquake wasn't it.

✤ ✤ ✤

Time has a way of passing so quickly.

So quickly indeed.

One morning in the mid-1990s, as I looked in the mirror, I stopped shaving mid-stroke and stared at my face. My whiskers were graying. Deep, irreversible lines lay underneath my eyes. Long gone was the sleek, almost gaunt visage of my youth. Middle age had arrived, and I wondered where the years had gone.

The same years were slipping by for Shayla too. She had become a principal by then at Amboy Middle School, home of the mighty Eagles. The small town of Amboy was located in a quiet, rural setting, maybe half an hour from the Columbia River. Shayla told me she enjoyed the commute to and from school on the winding, leafy backwoods roads. Her big Lincoln really hugged the corners, she added, making her feel safe and secure.

We stayed in touch through letters and phone calls. Each year I'd still go up and visit the family for a few days. Dave and I hiked in the forest and marveled at the deer that meandered by, and Shayla and I talked for hours between ourselves. Shayla still grew as many flowers as she could—copious rose and dahlia gardens, and she gave out flowers freely to anyone she met. She loved to feed people, and we ate sumptuous meals together as a family, breakfasts with platters of pancakes, melted butter, and hot maple syrup, steaming sausages and eggs, lunches with all the trimmings, dinners with laughter and wine.

Shayla excelled at her job and was well known and loved throughout the seventeen schools of the Battle Ground School District. Whenever she went on holiday, she brought back gifts for all the teachers and staff at her school. She helped plan the construction of a new school building at Amboy and gave careful attention to its layout. She insisted on a lot of light and windows—"No darkness anywhere" was her mandate. She sent me several photos of the new school when it was finished, including a shot of the entry-way—the picture showed warm and welcoming entry doors with a North-west log cabin–styled peaked roof, just perfect for the location. Right from moment one, she wanted every student to feel like he or she belonged at the new school, she said.

The light and windows reflected the peace and passion that Shayla felt in her soul in her middle age, I believe. From the stories she told me, and the many newspaper clippings I read about her, she was a powerhouse of love and care to all she met, a tireless, colossal advocate for children. She established her own personal, private charity, called the Shayla Ebner Fund for Kids, or Shayla's Purse for short, which was basically just her dipping into her own pocket anytime she found out a student needed something that the child's parents couldn't afford. Shayla was always buying a new pair of shoes for a child at her school, a winter coat, a backpack, a haircut, a new notebook. She governed her school with one fundamental question: "Is it good for the kids?" And kids, parents, teachers, district officials, and even area journalists praised her for her fairness, compassion, and top educational results achieved. She was especially pleased when her school earned the prestigious School of Distinction award from the state and became a presidential Blue Ribbon School.

One time when I was up at their house, I noticed tucked away on a shelf my old motorcycle helmet, the one I'd been wearing during my crash. The shell was cracked in several places, and anyone could see the helmet had been through a bad accident. I asked Shayla how she'd come to have this possession of mine, and she just gave me a quizzical smile and said she'd taken it home after visiting me in the hospital in Oregon.

I didn't pry further about why she'd taken the helmet, or what it meant to her, or what greater meaning the helmet possibly had within her spirit. But later on in conversation she inferred that she was grateful for that helmet, and the hand it had played in saving my life. It was a marker of God's protection, she said, and it brought her a feeling of comfort to have it around. So that was that.

These were such seasons of brightness—they radiated the love that I had for this family, and they had for me.

Little Shaylita (whose name really is just Shayla, but I can't stop calling her Shaylita, no matter how old she gets) grew up and fell in love and got engaged to a guy named Tony, and I was asked to perform the wedding ceremony. They wanted to hold it in the vacation destination of Bend, Oregon, about three hours from Portland, and we made arrangements with a church in Bend. Shaylita's fiancé was not Catholic, and I understood he felt some concern at meeting a priest and having a Catholic wedding. As soon as I met Tony, I knew he was a solid, stand up guy. We smoked cigars together and had a taste of single malt outside on the porch, and I said, "Communication is the key to any good marriage," and he said, "You're right." And we got along well from that moment forward.

Two years later, Davida got married. She wanted an outdoor wedding, and the only place we could find was at an outdoor sanctuary called the Grotto in Portland, Oregon. The Grotto is a beautiful sixty-two acre botanical garden built right within the heart of the northeastern corner of the city.

The gardens have grown up around an old stone church. Staff at the Grotto only allow one wedding a week on church property, which primarily serves as a sanctuary for reflection and prayer, but we were able to squeeze Davida and Patrick's wedding into their schedule. Portland is often rainy, but the weather on their wedding day was perfect.

I felt honored, again, to be part of these two momentous celebrations in this family's life. I couldn't have been more proud if the brides had been my own daughters.

One evening when I was over at Shayla and Dave's house, we all stayed up late talking. The girls were both married and on their own by then, and it was just the three of us alone in the house now. Dave needed to work early the next morning, so he went to bed after a while. The house was quiet then, and Shayla and I sat in the living room, me in the recliner, her on the sofa, and I looked at her hard out of the corner of my eye without saying anything. I had that questioning feeling that can sometimes come along when a person has known a friend for such a long time, but I struggled to form words around the question, so I kept my mouth shut. I recognized it as that desire to name something, wanting to articulate what Shayla was to me, and me to her.

I studied Shayla more closely. She was as middle aged as I was, yet still as fair as the sun, bright as the stars in procession. There were laugh lines around her eyes and across her forehead when she smiled, and her youthfulness had been replaced by elements of practicality. But she was still beautiful; that much was clear to me. I'd need to be blind not to see it. She wore brown pants and a pale-colored top, and her hair was still short, although there were flecks of gray in it now. She had figured out life; that's the conclusion I came to. She knew what truly mattered. And I came to a second conclusion: We weren't simply friends. No, we were long past that terminology. We were family in a sense, but not exactly, not quite. We weren't lovers, nor did the temptation of a physical relationship at our stage of life enter the picture. The youthful passion we had felt for each other when we were younger had been replaced by something deeper. The word flew into my mind in a rush.

Devotion.

I was devoted to Shayla, and she was devoted to me.

Our love contained elements of ardency, of duty and faithfulness, of affection and fondness and consecration and concern. We were not "wild" about each other—a term like that was reserved for teenagers and lovers. We didn't "dote" on each other—a term like that was for senior citizens after a lifetime of marriage. She was simply Shayla, and I was simply Norm. And we were devoted to each other—always.

The question was settled in my mind. I didn't say anything to Shayla about it. Instead, I simply said good night, and she to me.

She went to her bedroom with Dave, and I went to my bedroom to pray. We didn't know it at the moment, but the storm was right around the corner. Prayer would become our lifeline then. God would become all we could cling to, all we knew to be certain and sure.

CHAPTER 11

The Worst News Ever

AFTER EIGHT YEARS OF FRUITFUL MINISTRY in Fillmore, I drove out of the town for the last time as a resident, heading for a new ministry in Santa Clarita, a larger city on the northern edge of Greater Los Angeles. Change again— always the natural shyness to be gulped down and the pledge to be renewed before God to reach outside myself.

The church I was assigned to was called Our Lady of Perpetual Help, and soon the ministry there turned difficult. I'd been a senior pastor in Fillmore for several years by then, and felt comfortable in that role, but I was made an associate pastor at Our Lady, which at first felt like a demotion of sorts, although God's service holds no real hierarchy. The pope is just as much a servant of the Lord as a brand new priest. The more I thought about it, the move back to associate minister was actually a relief because I didn't have to be concerned about finances, personnel, or upkeep of the facilities like I did back in Fillmore.

I was told that when the pastor retired I would become the new senior pastor, but I wasn't sure if I wanted that. If I wasn't the senior pastor, then I could spend more time serving people. Fortunately I didn't need to make the decision. When the senior pastor retired, a committee of priests from the Archdiocese was formed to hire his replacement, and they ended up hiring one of their committee members for the position instead. He was an okay guy, but overall he had a different vision for ministry than I did, and increasingly I became uncomfortable under his leadership. I felt limited in what I could do, and that didn't settle well in my soul.

In the midst of all this, ministry continued. I became active in ministering to the gangs again. There was a horrific gang shooting in the nearby town of Newhall, done by a gangster from Val Verde, and immediately a lot of talk surfaced about the other gang seeking revenge. I secured permission to close the streets and hold a service right there out in the open on the street where the shooting had taken place. I implored the people in my hearing to find a peaceful solution to work this out. The people agreed, and no revenge killings took place.

Another associate priest at Santa Clarita, Father Malcolm, became a dear friend. One day he asked a favor. A relative of his worked for a company that led tours in Israel. They wanted a priest to accompany them, but Father Malcolm was not interested, so he asked me. I went once and everything went well, so I ended up helping lead tours with them for the next ten years. Every other year we went to Israel. The other years we went to Italy, France and Portugal, the Czech Republic and Poland, Germany and Switzerland, Greece and Turkey. Sometimes when we went to the Holy Land we also went to Egypt. On each trip I felt God watching over us.

One time in Germany the people in the group were nervous because there were terrible storms all around us. In the midst of the storms, we attended a showing of the Passion play in Oberammergau, and I told our people that God's spirit was watching over us despite the threatening weather. Before the play began, a dove flew overhead and landed on my shoulder. He stayed with me, perfectly at peace, and I was able to hold the bird on the back of my hand for some time. The dove would not go to anyone else, even though many tried to coax it over. When the curtain lifted and the play began, the dove flew away and disappeared on the horizon. People said later that after that experience they were confident of God's presence on the trip.

During the six years I spent at Our Lady, I continued leading the mission church in Val Verde and started another mission church in the small town of Castaic. My leadership responsibilities in those places felt to me like I was doing something purposeful, bringing places of worship and gathering to areas that didn't have them before. But despite these successes, I increasingly felt burdened to move on. I applied for a reassignment and was given one. But my new location surprised me.

It was 2002 when the transfer came through. I was sixty years old by then, and I was given the position of chaplain at Bishop Alemany High School in Mission Hills. Again, I was to work with teenagers. Previously, they had two priests at the school, and they'd both been reassigned. At first I said, "I'm too old. You should have a young priest working with youth." But they said, "No, you're the man for the job." So I accepted. Funny, the twists that life can throw at a person.

The day I left Our Lady, I was packing up my car to leave, and I placed my chalice—the silver one with the gold insides that we'd made as a family when I was ordained—on top of a pile of boxes in the backseat of my car and went inside to gather another load. I left my car doors open for sake of convenience, and when I returned, the chalice was gone. It hadn't fallen anywhere in the car. A few other possessions were missing, and I could tell right away I'd been robbed. The chalice was priceless to me, filled with personal value from years of use, but there was nothing I could do. I didn't say anything to anyone. I prayed about it silently, then drove over to my new assignment at Alemany.

Two weeks later, I received a call from the parish at Our Lady. The administrator asked if I was missing anything.

"Well, yes, actually," I replied. "My chalice."

The administrator was quiet on the other end for a moment, then said, "I've got good news for you."

A family had been out walking a few mornings earlier down by the Santa Clarita River and had seen something gleaming in the sand. At first they thought it was an earring. Only a speck of metal was visible in the silt. One of the family members went over, uncovered it, and saw that the gleam came from something much larger than a piece of jewelry.

The odds of finding my chalice in the river were unfathomable. The Santa Clarita River is more than eighty miles long, one of the largest river systems along the coast of Southern California. The bottom and sides of most rivers in this arid region have been lined with concrete to preserve every precious drop of water, but the Santa Clarita is one of the few that's still lined with its original shifting, moving, swallowing sand.

The chalice had only the name of Christ and my name on it, as well as a cross made from my mother's rings. There was no address or other identifying markers that anyone would know except me. In the Santa Clarita area, there are more than two hundred churches, yet this family took that chalice straight to the very same parish that I'd just been at—Our Lady of Perpetual Help—knocked on the door, and asked if anyone knew who it belonged to.

This family wasn't Catholic. They had no connections with anyone in the church. From the location in the river where they described finding my chalice, I realized they weren't even nearest to the parish of Our Lady. Other parishes were closer. Still, for some reason, they took it back to the very same parish where I'd just been working.

I've never met this family to thank them. I've always wondered what they looked like. I wanted to shake their hands and let them know what their find meant to me. But for some odd reason, the administrator didn't think to take down their contact information. I've wondered over the years if maybe that oversight was guided by some unseen Hand. Maybe this was a family of angels. In a world that holds forth much wonder and mystery, stranger things have happened. However it can be explained or not explained, the return of my chalice felt personal to me. It felt as if God had reached out to endorse again His calling on my life to be a father to many.

Very quickly I grew to love my new job at the high school. With my years of background in youth ministry and at the retreats, Bishop Alemany proved to be a natural fit. Immediately, I started holding retreats for the teens—on friendship, choices, discipleship, and God's timing in their lives. I learned names and met parents. I grew to genuinely love the teens I served at the school.

A year passed and then another, and then another, and another, and the days took on a pleasant and purposeful rhythm. I counseled students and listened to their concerns. I gave them high fives as I passed them in the hallways, and they me. I attended their plays, band concerts, football games, volleyball games, water polo games, soccer matches, and track meets. I spoke and prayed at their graduation ceremonies and baccalaureates. I cheered at their art festivals and debate tournaments.

One day a man came to visit me at the school. He wasn't a student at Bishop Alemany, and I couldn't place him, but somehow he'd tracked me down and knew my name. I estimated him to be in his early twenties, with a solid build and a firm handshake, maybe weighing 180 pounds.

Right off, he asked me if I recognized him, and I replied that I didn't. He said with a grin, "Rightfully so." He explained that back when I was ministering in Fillmore, I'd come to visit him in the hospital. He'd weighed only 90 pounds then and was dying of AIDS. Time was short for this young man, and I'd anointed him with oil and prayed for him.

"Do you remember what you specifically prayed for me?" the man asked.

I shook my head. "Not specifically, no."

"You prayed that I would be blessed, you prayed that I'd draw closer to God, and you prayed for my healing," he said. "After you left the room, I felt something go through me that felt like fire. Right away—in that moment—I knew I was healed. I told the doctor that, but he didn't believe me. He insisted I was still dying. So I told him to give me another AIDS test. He said he wouldn't, that another test was only a waste of money. But I persisted until he administered the test, and sure enough I was completely clean of AIDS. I'm in perfect health today."

I hugged the young man. We marveled together at how God sometimes chooses to work. I prayed with him again, shook his hand again, and he left. That was the last time I saw him.

Not long after that, one of the students at Alemany asked to speak with me. Her father was dying of cancer, she said. Would I pray for him? So I did. He came to a chapel service at our school, and we gathered together as students and staff and all prayed together. About a week later, the man visited his doctor. The cancer was gone.

Over the years I have witnessed many other remarkable healings besides the ones I've mentioned in this book. I believe this is true: that God always heals when we ask that of Him through prayer. It might not be physical healing that comes. It can be emotional healing, or spiritual healing, or mental healing, or psychological healing. But God always heals. Always.

Throughout the years I've prayed for sick people, and their physical sicknesses haven't always vanished. It fact, it's the rare exception when they do. It's not like I have any special powers myself, and I do not understand the mind of God in these complicated matters. But when I pray for people, I always see some sort of healing.

Sometimes I simply see a person relax as I pray. His or her mind has been scrambled because of the pain of the sickness, or perhaps the person's mind and soul are twisted with anxiety and uncertainty. The mind clears and the body goes calm, like a lake after a storm.

❧ ❧ ❧

I reminded myself in big ways of this truth—that God always heals—starting in November 2011, when Shaylita's first baby was born, a daughter named Morgan, Shayla and Dave's first grandchild. She was a fine, healthy baby, and her face, eyes, cheeks, and mouth looked to be a perfect mixture of her father's and mother's features. Everyone was so proud.

Yet, in the midst of this season of excitement and hope, it felt as if a fly buzzed around the inside of Shayla's house, a seemingly minor annoyance that wouldn't go away. That annoyance consisted of some white spots underneath Shayla's tongue that showed up and wouldn't leave. Shayla called and almost as an afterthought filled me in on the news.

Shayla's life was extremely busy with work and family. She couldn't be bothered by such nuisances, and she'd always been healthy and seldom had gone to the doctor. Yet a month after her grandchild was born, on December 30, 2011, the day before New Year's Eve, the fly was still buzzing. So Shayla had the spots checked out by a doctor just to be on the safe side. He prescribed an antifungal medicine and did a biopsy. In the middle of January, a month of wintery cold, word came back.

Shayla had throat cancer.

No initial prognosis was given. Doctors soon did surgery to remove a small tumor on the floor of her mouth. They typed it and classified it and got all of it. They also did another procedure, this one longer, where they cut into her neck and went up under her ears and removed lymph nodes. It was supposed to be a two-hour surgery, but as they progressed they didn't like what they were seeing and kept on going deeper and deeper. A full ten and a half hours later, the surgery was finished. When the report came back, it showed they'd taken out twenty-seven nodes. Nineteen contained cancer. We all knew at this point that the news was very serious. Oncologists recommended both chemotherapy and radiation immediately. Shayla knew the treatments would be rough, but she agreed.

She vowed to fight this with everything she had.

All kinds of feelings gripped me when I received this news. Overall, I found the news frightening. I wondered if the doctors could cure Shayla's cancer, or if her condition would be fatal. Fear clouded my faith; I admit it. I sensed anew how short our lives are. In this strange, lifelong devotion I had to Shayla, I'd always known one of us would die first—whether she before me, or me before her—and I'd always imagined it would be me, but now I wasn't so certain. When I got the news, I immediately dropped to my knees in my office at the school and prayed for Shayla's healing.

I didn't want to let her go. I didn't want her to leave.

I prayed for Dave too. He and Shayla had been married a long time, and I knew this new season of their lives was going to be difficult for them both. They'd developed a strong symbiotic relationship over the years, a relationship where they each depended on the other. Dave handled the day-to-day living questions—who would pay the bills—that sort of thing. Shayla took care of friendships and relationships—writing the cards, making the phone calls, having people over for dinner. Dave tended not to talk about things. Shayla would make sure things got talked about. Their talents, gifts, and temperaments combined well.

I groaned, thinking how hard this would be on the girls. They had such a strong relationship with their mother. Shayla always helped them look into where they were at, what they were feeling, and what was going on in their lives.

From then on, every morning and evening I prayed for Shayla and the family. I prayed for Shayla throughout the day, too, whenever she came to mind, which seemed to be all the time those days. With each message received from Shayla or any of the family members, I rode a roller coaster of hope and disappointment depending on the news received.

The radiation focused on both her mouth and neck. The pace was grueling. Shayla went five days a week, week after week, and received a total of thirty-three treatments. At the end of the sessions, her mouth and esophagus were fried. She couldn't eat or talk. They admitted her to the hospital where a tube was inserted into her stomach. For five days she wavered, then began to show signs of improvement, so she went home to rest. After about three weeks she could talk and eat again. During all this time she kept up with a single infusion of chemotherapy once a week.

At the end of the treatments more scans were done, and at first all looked good: The cancer was held at bay. We all let out a collective sigh of relief. For six splendid weeks during the summer of 2012, Shayla relaxed. She gardened whenever she felt well enough. She cooed over her new granddaughter. She played with her two beloved Weimaraners, Lilly and Lucy.

I came up and visited during those wonderful weeks. Shayla looked to be her same radiant self, except more tired than usual, and she told me she felt weak. We had several long conversations, and it was in many ways like old times, except that before I left I gave her the blessing of the sick, the Catholic sacrament for healing. I anointed her forehead with oil and prayed, asking God to bless her, watch over her, and remove this disease from her life.

She soon saw a variety of doctors for follow up visits. Then a doctor found a small node in her neck. They biopsied it right away, and for two days we all held our breath. The results came back.

The cancer had returned.

More tests were administered, and the news came back even worse. The cancer had spread to Shayla's lungs and spine, as well as a handful of lymph nodes. It was August when I heard this news, and it was hot in Los Angeles. Day after day, the heavy Santa Ana winds blew from the east across the city like massive hair dryers turned on high. Alone one morning in prayer, I begged God for healing. A peace came into my soul, yes, but I still felt a sense of uneasiness. I knew Shayla's life was in the hands of the God of all comfort, the God of all peace. It wasn't an absence of problems that God promises to those who believe. It was the knowledge that He provides.

I phoned Shayla, and she asked me to read her some Scripture over the phone. I started in Isaiah 41:10, where God says simply, "Fear not, for I am with you." Then I thumbed over a few pages to Isaiah 43, where God promises that He will be with us whenever we pass though deep waters or raging fires. Then I took her to Isaiah 49, where in the sixteenth verse God declares that He has written our names on the palms of His hands. God will never forget us, much the same way a mother would never forget a baby nursing at her breast. Shayla thanked me, and we prayed together over the phone.

After that, there was silence for a few days. The next news landed like a blow to the side of the head.

The cancer was spreading so quickly, oncologists were worried that Shayla wouldn't last until Christmas. They told her how they could give her a targeted chemotherapy. It wouldn't be a traditional type of chemotherapy that would kill everything and ultimately help her heal, they said, but the targeted chemo at least would buy her some more time. When I talked to her on the phone next, I asked her how much.

"About a year," Shayla said. Her voice sounded strangely buoyant.

Shayla started receiving the targeted chemo. In September she felt okay, so the family traveled to see Dave's relatives in Nantucket. She described how the trip felt good, but a sense of heaviness clouded the visit, too. Nobody knew exactly what kind of time Shayla had left. She was constantly losing weight. Her first chemo had made her hair fall out, but this new type of chemo actually grew hair, and Shayla's hair returned, full and curly. She kept it cut short as always.

Shayla continued with the chemo. The roller coaster continued. They did another scan and received great news! Her lungs and spine were cleared.

But bad news came with it too —two lymph nodes still had cancer. And there was a new spot on her left arm.

Shayla felt a lot of pain in her arm, so she had some radiation treatments there—not to kill the cancer, but to treat the pain. After the treatments, unfortunately, her arm felt worse, not better. The bone was weakened, and her arm broke spontaneously, perhaps while she rolled over at night in her sleep. Surgeons operated and put a rod in her arm, and they did some more tests. They found some more cancer in her arm. They did a partial shoulder replacement, trying to help her and ease the situation. Hard news just kept landing, worse and worse.

Anytime I spoke with Shayla on the phone, she remained upbeat and optimistic, although realistic too. Dave told me how she was the hospital staff's favorite, always encouraging them and speaking kindly to them. She brought them little presents. They loved having her around. Shayla tried to remain as independent as possible. She made her own doctors' appointments and drove over and back on the days she felt okay to do so. But around then, Dave described how Shayla started to ask him to drive her more. She felt weaker, more unstable. She didn't feel safe driving herself anymore.

She was still working at the middle school. She tried to retire once, but the superintendent asked her to come back on the days she felt okay. Shayla agreed. She loved being around the kids. Her school was a well-oiled machine by then, and much of the school could run itself with the staff she had in place. Besides that, everybody just loved having her around.

In the spring of 2013, Shayla needed to stop her chemo treatments because they weren't working anymore. Oncologists started her on another drug, but it made her sick. So they tried another drug, and this one worked, at first quite well.

On the Fourth of July, 2013, Shayla called me with the fantastic news that she'd had a clear scan, her first in a long while. The roller coaster climbed to the highest peak. Oh, we were ecstatic. Everybody was. The news gave me chills. It meant that although the cancer wasn't necessarily gone, no cancer was showing up anywhere in her body. There were no tumors. No spots. Nothing. For the first time in a long while, we started talking about her beating this. Like it might only be a chronic disease, not a life-threatening one.

For the first time in a long while, everybody was happy again.

❦ ❦ ❦

I reminded myself of this truth—that God always heals—one afternoon a few weeks later, in August 2013.

I was seventy-one years old—I couldn't believe my senior years had crept up so quickly already—and we were holding a health fair at our church. A variety of free medical services were offered—blood sugar testing, blood pressure checks, free sonograms of the carotid arteries (a test that can show early signs of heart disease and other illnesses)—that type of thing. So I had a variety of tests done, and when I had the sonogram of my neck, the technician discovered something he didn't like the look of. He checked all around my throat and found two spots on my thyroid, so he gave me the images from the sonogram and told me to make an appointment with my doctor as quickly as possible.

I went to the doctor's office, and my doctor just happened to be walking through the lobby at the exact moment I arrived. I showed her the picture, without even having an appointment, and she said, "Come right up to my office." So they biopsied it, and sure enough there were not two but three little spots on my thyroid. They stuck needles in and got the results, and sure enough, those spots were cancerous.

I had cancer too.

Well, holy smash—I didn't like the sound of that whatsoever. For the second time in my life—the first time being my motorcycle accident—I felt the dark finger of mortality beckoning. It felt oddly coincidental to have cancer in my neck, the same area of the body where Shayla's had begun. A slew of thoughts flooded through my mind. Our lives had always been so close, but now this? I envisioned myself going through the same chemotherapy and radiation, having multiple surgeries, riding the roller coaster of news up and down.

I called Shayla and told her the news. She said she'd pray for me, and I promised to continue praying for her. I expressed that I wanted to come up and see her soon, and she said yes, to come up as soon as I could. Dave wanted to see me too. We talked about mortality a bit, about how death was so certain in this life for everybody. Shayla said she enjoyed her life so much, she'd love to continue to work with the children at the school and see her grandchildren grow, but if it was time for her to go, then she felt she had used her life well. She was ready.

We talked about how death isn't meant to be feared, about how John 14:3 gives us great comfort. In that passage, Jesus has promised to prepare a place for us in his Father's house. By faith, we are all welcome in God's house. We also talked about my motorcycle accident when I felt ready to go to God, but God was not through with me yet. Shayla believed that was the same situation in my life today— that God still had much more work for me to do, and I wasn't going to die yet. But when it came to her, she believed her respite was going to be a short one, and that God was calling her to be with the people she had loved who had gone before.

They set up an operation for October 3 and took out my thyroid. I prayed for healing, sure, and I invited a lot of other people to pray for me too. Many of them did.

Fortunately, all my cancer was removed in that one operation. Doctors had big grins on their faces after it was over. The operation was a tremendous success. It was so successful, even, that I didn't need any other treatments.

No chemotherapy. No radiation. No drugs except a thyroid replacement. I was completely cured of cancer.

That was good news. But unfortunately I couldn't muster much happiness just then.

A day or so later, after my surgery, after my scans, Shayla called me to ask how it all had gone.

"Really well," I told her. "Better than anyone expected. My cancer's gone, Shayla. Completely gone." My tone of voice was steady. My news was good, but I was sensitive to what she was going through too.

"I'm so happy for you, Norm," she said. "Sincerely—so happy with the news." She paused, then added that she was so happy my cancer had not been as serious or devastating as hers. We both promised to pray for each other and to continue to trust God.

I asked her what the news was from her end.

"I don't know if I want to talk about me right now," she said.

"It's okay," I answered, but I still pressed her for an update. I don't know if that was a mistake or not. But Shayla was always forthright. She wasn't one to hide anything from me, and we both knew that.

"Well, doctors are saying I won't get through this," Shayla said simply.

We were quiet on the phone after that. Neither of us hung up. But we didn't say anything either.

CHAPTER 12

Where Rose Gardens Once Bloomed

ON THE LAST WEEKEND OF SEPTEMBER 2013, some friends were at the house visiting Shayla and Dave. Shayla was having a hard time breathing. Dave took her to the hospital. Doctors did an X-ray and saw a large amount of fluid in her lungs. They removed as much fluid as they could and hospitalized her. Doctors didn't see any cancer in the fluid they pulled from her, which would have been an indication of a tumor, so they sent her home. We all breathed a sigh of relief.

Shayla set a goal of taking her grandchildren to Disneyland. A trip was planned for December. But one complication set in, and then another, and then another, and then another. It seemed like Shayla just couldn't get ahead. They did a scan and discovered a small tumor in the bottom of one lung.

The cancer had returned, and the prognosis wasn't good. Disneyland would need to wait.

Her lungs filled with fluid again. Again, they drained her lungs. Shaylita and her husband planned to go to Bend, Oregon, near the end of October to celebrate their tenth wedding anniversary. Family members were invited along. Shayla really wanted to go too, and she told the doctors, "Just do whatever you need to do to make me comfortable enough for a few days." They pumped her full of medication.

Shayla traveled the three hours by car to Bend, and when she got to the hotel she immediately went upstairs and to bed. Family members described how something looked to be changing very rapidly right in front of them. That was a Friday night.

Early on Saturday morning, Shayla began to throw up. She grew too weak to walk downstairs by herself. Dave and Shaylita's husband carried her downstairs and put her in the car for the drive back to a hospital in Portland. Shayla stayed in the hospital for five days. Doctors did whatever they could think of for her.

Then, there was no more they could do, the doctors said. Nothing at all. So Shayla went home.

She wanted to be in the house that Dave had built for her. She wanted to be where they had raised their children. She wanted to be near the land where deer walked the trails to the river, where rose gardens once bloomed.

Dave set up a hospital bed downstairs. Shayla wasn't sure at first if she was going to use it or not. She liked her own bed. But she said it looked pretty comfortable, so that's where she stayed. Dave started sleeping downstairs too, to be near her.

A few days later, when Dave phoned me, he didn't talk much. He said simply, "Come see Shayla one more time. Come as quickly as you can."

I set down my phone after he hung up and looked around my office. It was one of those blank moments in my mind, the clock on the wall ticking in my ears, where the things that normally stare you in the face don't look the same as they always do. On my office walls are eight different paintings of Jesus. People have given them to me over the years. There are plaques and awards. Pictures of weddings I've done. Masses I've celebrated. My shelves are piled with books. I keep a pet cockatiel named Happy in my office, and he chirped and squawked as normal. But everything was different. Everything was about to change.

I snapped into action, found and booked a plane ticket online, made a few phone calls to organize my schedule, then went home to pack a few things. Just before I left for the airport, I stood outside the rectory by my Toyota Prius and took one last look around.

Across the street were some boys playing soccer. They paused in the action, smiled and waved, and I waved back. Duchess, the friendly neighborhood dog who belongs to a retired priest who lives nearby, wagged her tail in my direction and gave me a sociable yelp. Some girls were practicing a dance on the sidewalk in front of the church. They greeted me in Spanish, and I smiled and waved. Just everyday scenes of normalcy around the parish grounds.

Then I took a deep breath, climbed in my car, and headed to the airport.

☙ ☙ ☙

Dave picked me up at the airport and filled me in on Shayla's condition. It was evening when we arrived back at their house. Shayla was taking a lot of painkillers but she was lucid. She lay on the hospital bed in their living room. I hugged Shayla when I came in, and we made some small talk and caught up a bit. She soon grew sleepy, and it was late. We promised to talk more in the morning, and we said good night. I went to the guest bedroom close by.

That night in my dreams, a mass of images swirled together. When a knock sounded on my door and all was dark, I needed to check myself at first to see if I wasn't still dreaming. The knock came again. I looked at my watch; it was 4:00 a.m. I roused myself and answered the door.

Dave stood before me. His eyes were puffy, and he looked tired. I wondered if he'd slept at all that night. "Shayla wants to go to confession," he said. "After that, she wants to talk with you one more time."

I nodded, slid on a pair of pants and a shirt, and came over to where Shayla lay on the hospital bed. Dave walked upstairs to get a little more sleep. Shayla and I were left alone. I sat by her bed. She smiled at me, and I nodded. Her breaths came shallow and she needed to pause between words.

Slowly, Shayla began the familiar words. "In the name of the Father . . . and of the Son . . . and of the Holy Spirit." She named the time of her last confession. I read to her a few passages from Scripture. She confessed her sins and told God she was sorry. I assigned no penance but only asked her to pray for her family, then led her in an act of contrition—a prayer for forgiveness. I recited the words of absolution, the familiar phrases to remind a hearer that God always forgives. And then the formalities were over. I knew these acts were important to her faith.

We looked at each other for a while. This time I would speak boldly. I would take all I'd ever learned from Shayla about speaking first, about truth in speaking, about directness and genuineness of speech and deed.

"Shayla," I said. "I still love you very much."

She swallowed. Her throat sounded dry, the contraction labored. "Norm," she said. "I still love you … very much too."

I wasn't quite sure how to get out the words I wanted to say next, or if I could quite convey what I wanted to ask her. I just wanted to make sure everything was right between us, so I said, "If there's anything I ever did to hurt you, I'm so sorry."

Her words came quicker this time. "You never did anything … to hurt me."

I tried to smile. "I'm angry about one thing, though," I said. "I was supposed to go home to God first. I was supposed to give you a big hug when you got to heaven and welcome *you* home."

The corner of her mouth flickered into a grin. "You don't know that … Norm. Your plane might crash on the way home … You'll get the opportunity … to welcome me then." She was kidding. It was her last joke with me.

She asked me to make a list. The list was already in her mind, but she didn't have the strength to write. I found a pen and notepad, and she recited the names of all the people she loved and cared about. She wanted to make sure the people knew when she passed, and that they were invited to the funeral. When she was finished, the list had reached many pages.

Then Shayla closed her eyes. Her breathing was slow, and she was at peace. She fell asleep.

And she was still breathing when I stole out of the room.

🌿 🌿 🌿

It was a few weeks later, November 22, 2013, a beautiful, crisp autumn day in the Pacific Northwest, and Shayla had been living with cancer for a year and ten months.

She was still at home, now under hospice care, and she was under low doses of morphine to ease her pain, still having difficulty swallowing. That morning, she said she was very thirsty, and she asked for water. She hadn't been asking for anything lately. Dave and Shaylita were at the house, and Dave got her some. Davida was in San Francisco on business, and Shaylita telephoned Davida and relayed the news: The roller coaster was heading downhill. Davida jumped on the next plane and was home in Washington in a few hours.

That afternoon, one by one, Shayla called each family member over to her bedside to say good-bye. It was a quiet, methodical work of love. Shayla's mind was fully functioning, and family members were certain she knew exactly what she was doing. After she had finished saying good-bye to each person, she asked everyone to come over together so she could say one last thing to everybody.

"I know . . . I'm dying," Shayla said. "And I'm ready to die . . . I want you all to go on living. I want you to go on loving each other, being kind to each other . . . taking care of each other. I really love you all." When she was done, she drifted off to sleep.

That night, family members took turns watching over her.

The next day, November 23, was a Saturday, another beautiful fall day. In the afternoon, Dave went out and mowed the lawn. The hospice service called to see how Shayla was doing. In many ways, it felt like a normal day. When Dave finished the lawn, he drove to the pharmacy to pick up a prescription.

The living room Shayla was lying in has floor-to-ceiling glass that over-looks the river and hillside. The sun sets early in November, maybe 4:30 or 5:00 o'clock, and the sun began to set through the windows. Shaylita's hus-band, Tony, was taking a turn watching Shayla. He called everyone into the room. "Something's changing," he said.

Shaylita phoned her dad and told him to forget the prescription. He needed to hurry home. Then she walked over to her mother and said, "Dad's not here. Don't leave us yet."

As if by a force of will, Shayla's breathing changed again, and it went back to normal.

Dave got home. Shaylita's husband took their child out of the house, so it was just Shaylita, Davida, and Dave in the room with her. They sat around Shayla's bed, holding her hands, stroking her forehead. One by one they told her how much they loved her.

Shayla's breaths grew further and further apart.

Finally, there was only one breath. One last gulp of earth's oxygen.

Then Shayla passed, and began breathing the new air of heaven's paradise.

⚜ ⚜ ⚜

Dave phoned me not long after that.

"I've one final request to make of you, Norm," he said.

"Anything," I answered quickly.

"Will you . . ." and here he broke. He paused for a moment, then added, "Will you come up and do Shayla's funeral?"

CHAPTER 13

Something Important about Cars

WHEN THE TIME CAME FOR THE MEMORIAL SERVICE, I flew up to Washington State again. As I flew, my mind filled with memories of the special people I had lost over the years. Many people. I remembered my mom calling me in the early morning in 1988 when my father died in his sleep, and seeing his body so still and cold at their house. I remembered my sister Janet at only forty-nine years old telling us she was going to die from cancer. I asked what she wanted for her last birthday. She answered, "Flowers," so all of us family members and cousins got together and sent her fifty bouquets of flowers. I was up in Redding with her and took pictures of the big smile she had. Then I watched my mother as I visited her every week slowly go downhill and finally pass into eternal life. There was another very important person gone from me.

Dave picked me up at the airport and drove me back to their home. It was strangely quiet now in Dave and Shayla's house. An important piece was missing— so glaringly missing. They had been married for forty-three years.

That evening, Dave and I talked extensively through the details of the service and the pieces the family wanted included. We talked about the tone and the feel, about the specific readings she wanted, about who would do what and when. It felt like we needed to speak quietly, carefully.

On the morning of the funeral, I rose early, showered, dressed, and prayed, then went for a short walk around the property. The crispness of December lay in the air. The ground all around their home felt heavy with frost, and the deer trail down to the river felt icy and dangerous to walk on. I turned around soon and headed back to the warmth of the kitchen where I poured myself a cup of coffee, trying to get a handle on my feelings.

I knew I was grieving deeply, for my own loss as well as for the family's. Anytime I glanced in Dave's direction, I could see the pain in his face. He loved Shayla truly and deeply, and I was grateful he had been such an important person in her life. They had built so many things together—a home, a family, so many memories—and now he had lost his lifelong companion. Life was going to change radically for Dave without his wife, and I understood that. I could only try to be with him as a brother in sorrow.

I grieved for the girls. They'd lost their mother, the one who gave birth to them, nursed them tenderly, cared for them as they grew, guided them into adulthood, all the while teaching them to face life with grace and courage. It was always clear to me that the girls loved their mother so closely, and she loved them. Her passing would be a huge loss to them, both now and in the years to come.

I grieved for the grandchildren. Shaylita and Tony had two children now. These children would not have the opportunity to grow up knowing the beautiful person who was their grandmother. They'd miss out on the guidance that only a grandmother can give. I wished very much that they could have known her and what she was like.

And I grieved for me. The loss of Shayla felt beyond words. I couldn't even begin to articulate the magnitude of what I was feeling. I couldn't get my hands around it and grab hold of it. This was Shayla, the Shayla I'd always known, the woman I was devoted to in love. The idea of leading her funeral was almost more than I could bear. But I wouldn't have wanted anybody else to do it. This was my responsibility—to help people celebrate her life. This was my privilege.

This was my ultimate joy.

🍁 🍁 🍁

When the time came for the funeral, we drove over to the Sacred Heart Catholic Church in the town of Battle Ground. Cars were already in the parking lot, and people were already filing inside.

The details were all taken care of. Instead of flowers, Shayla had requested that any gifts or donations be sent instead to the account at the local credit union for Shayla's Purse, the fund she had set up for needy children in her school district. A week after the memorial service at the church, another service was scheduled to be held in the gym at Amboy Middle School, where Shayla had been principal. Someone else would lead the service at the gym, and that was okay by me. Dave had known my schedule was tight, so he'd asked another family friend to lead that. Besides, I wasn't sure if I could emotionally handle both.

The church building was packed. Shayla had asked to be cremated, and the ceremony started with a traditional blessing of the ashes. A white cloth covered the urn, a remembrance of the white clothes Shayla wore when baptized as a baby and dedicated as a child of God. The symbolism behind the same color white being used in both a baby dedication and a funeral is that a person can always belong to God throughout that individual's entire life—from infancy to death.

We prayed as a congregation, and then we read from various passages of Scripture. First, we read from the book of Job in the Old Testament. He was an ancient follower of God who suffered one harsh blow after another. Toward the end of the book of Job, where Job has lost everything he's valued, he declares his undying trust in the goodness of God anyway. "I know that my Redeemer lives," Job said. "And after my skin has been destroyed, I shall see God." My mind trembled at the vision of Shayla's skin being destroyed by cancer, but something stilled my thoughts and I was able to speak about how no matter what hardships we face in this life, the same hope that Job held onto of God's goodness and provision is ours today. One day—as

Shayla was now doing—we would see God face-to-face. In His presence, everything would make sense then. Everything would be made right.

We read from Psalm 23, a passage familiar to so many people. *The Lord is my Shepherd, I shall not want. He makes me lie down in green pastures. He leads me beside still waters.* It almost seemed as if Jesus, the Good Shepherd himself, was reading the words straight into my heart. I heard God telling me that He walks alongside us in our journey throughout life. We all go through dark valleys, but even when we don't see God or feel His presence, He is always there, still watching over us, still guiding us, still caring for us. Eventually, as the psalm says, God will lead us to a place of rest.

And we read from the first letter of John, chapter 3, where the promise is repeated that one day we, the children of God, will see God. I wanted this truth to ring in the ears of all the people in the room. I wanted it to ring in my own ears, lest I ever forgot.

There were songs and music, and then Shaylita delivered the eulogy for her mother. She spoke of her mother's love of flowers, of roses, lilacs, and dahlias, of how she grew everything beautiful. Shayla used to go to Goodwill, where she bought vases. She gave away bucket loads of flowers to everyone she met.

Shaylita explained how her mother's entire life had been characterized by giving—even to strangers. She shared a story of an incident that happened one year at Christmastime. Shayla and Shaylita were at a department store, and on the way out they saw a man holding a sign. The man wasn't a panhandler. He was working for one of the stores, holding a "buy mattresses" sign, doing one of those jobs that can be fairly repetitive and thankless. Shayla stuck a twenty dollar bill in his jacket pocket and said, "You're doing a good job, keep it up. Merry Christmas." It was just a simple act of random kindness, yet those acts happened frequently whenever Shayla was around.

When it came time for my homily, I focused on Shayla's grandchildren, seated there in the service (I'd asked Shaylita earlier if I could use them as examples), and I talked about how there are three main stages to life.

The first stage lasts nine months. I motioned to the grandchildren and described how when each of them had been in the womb, they couldn't see anything, only darkness. They couldn't hear much, only the muffled sounds from the outside world. They ate only that which was passed through the umbilical cord. They had little opportunity for movement, and they could only travel where their mother took them. All went well for them in that stage of life, yet there was more goodness to come. Much more than they could ever imagine. They could not begin to grasp what life was like outside the womb.

The second stage of life arrives after we are born, I added. It's our life on earth from cradle to grave. "Imagine what it would be like," I said to the congregation, "if you tried to describe to a child in the womb what the second stage of life will be like. The child inside the womb has no vocabulary for it, no categories for picturing what the future will hold. You could try to describe the child's parents, what they look like, or what it will feel like to one day be soothed or nurtured by the mother or to be rocked in a crib-side chair at night by the father. Outside the womb, the child is going to see new and wonderful colors, shapes, patterns, and friendly faces. The child will one day meet amazing animals—barking dogs and meowing cats and funny turtles and playful guinea pigs. He'll make friends at church and school and will be able to play baseball, kick a soccer ball, and ride a skateboard. Imagine trying to describe a bicycle to a child in the womb. Or a jet ski. Or a university. One day, he will hear the music of guitars and drums and strings and woodwinds and will be able to dance. The child will be able to travel to amazing places—to Hawaii, to Disneyland, to the mountains, to the beach. He will taste a strawberry, a bowl of chocolate ice cream, a plate of spaghetti, the crisp tang of an orange. That child in the womb is not able to grasp the wonder that awaits. And yet it does await! It very much does."

The third stage of life comes after we die, I explained. I needed to pause and swallow. "It's eternity, forever, the life we spend with God, and it's every bit as real as the first two stages of life. If I were to tell you—"I gestured across the room—"that one day you will go to a place beyond anything you could ever imagine now, an entirely new home filled with mansions of gold, a new country of sights and sounds and smells and tastes and experiences beyond your wildest imagination, would you hold out hope in that direction? One day that will happen for everyone who seeks God through his mercy. We will see the God who made us. We will meet our loved ones from generations past who have gone before us. One day we will be in a place beyond anything we can imagine now. We have such limited understanding of it on this side of things, yet one day we will hear God's voice. We will dance to choirs of angels. We will taste heavenly food. We will live in a heavenly city. We will travel to new galaxies and dimensions beyond time and space. What we will experience for eternity will be so vastly beyond what we experience today."

"That's what Shayla is experiencing right now," I added. "There is no more cancer in her new reality. There is no more chemotherapy in her new home. No more radiation. No more heartache. No more suffering. No more sorrow. God has wiped away every tear from her eyes, and he has brought her to live with Him forever, in a home He prepared before the dawn of time for all who love Him and believe. That's what God has prepared for us, too. Just imagine the glory that awaits . . . We can only imagine."

I felt a silence within me, and I knew it was peace. I knew the words I had delivered were given to me by God. They were my last gift to Shayla.

⚜ ⚜ ⚜

A reception was held afterward. There were a lot of hugs and a lot of tears, yet a lot of smiles too. Laughter. Good memories told. Celebrating. Rejoicing.

Shayla wouldn't have wanted it any other way.

🌿 🌿 🌿

When I flew home, I looked out the airplane window at the gray clouds below and prayed again for the Ebner family. I knew that life had changed radically for them, that grief takes a long time to work through, and I wondered in what ways life would continue to change, and how they would remember this incredible woman over the next years to come. I had no answers for that yet, of course, and within those questions I wondered how life would change for me too. I knew I'd continue to remember Shayla always. But I didn't know exactly how.

A few parts were clear. There's a part of the Mass where we remember those who have died, and I knew I'd always bring her to mind and say a special prayer for her.

I knew I would talk about Shayla whenever I spoke about love at retreats and conferences.

I knew I still had the olive wood cross, the treasured gift Shayla had given me when she visited me in the hospital after my motorcycle accident, the cross that reminded us of love's sacrifices.

And I knew that whenever I would remember her, I would get tears in my eyes, like I had now as I looked out the window of the plane.

I blew my nose and put my handkerchief in my jacket pocket. It felt like there should be something more I could do. Some act of tribute maybe. A place I could go to. An act of service I could lead. A memorial that could be set up. I wasn't sure what, or where, or when, or how. But something felt unsettled still, like there was one last loose end in our relationship that still needed to be resolved. I knew Shayla wanted us all to keep living. I knew she wanted us all to keep going forward, to keep doing and being all God wanted. I knew she wanted me to stay true to my calling. To continue to be me.

When my plane landed in Los Angeles, I found my Prius in the parking lot and drove back to the rectory, still wondering. I am not one for seeing apparitions. I never seek to communicate with the dead. But as I drove, I swear I felt the presence of Shayla near me. Maybe it was only a memory of her, made alive only in my mind. Yet she felt so near me, so close to me, sitting right there in the seat next to me.

The memory caused me to smile, for in my mind Shayla was smiling warmly herself, gently patting the inside door frame like she sometimes did when we rode anywhere together. From her lips came speech. Maybe not audibly, maybe only to my spirit. Shayla was saying something I'd heard before. She was repeating what she'd said when we were young, although I couldn't quite recall the exact words at that moment.

It seemed, if I could discern this correctly, that she was assuring me that more would be revealed later. One last act of resolution would indeed happen, but it would happen the other way around—she would give a tribute to me, not me to her.

And, strangely enough, when I pressed in close to listen, it sounded like she was telling me something important about—did I hear this correctly?—*cars.*

CHAPTER 14

Limping, I Continue On

I NEEDED TO PUT THAT QUESTION ON HOLD for the time being. It would get answered shortly, in Shayla's time, in Shayla's way, but not quite yet. When I returned home from the memorial service, life hit again—all the responsibilities of being a full-time priest. Inwardly, I was in mourning for Shayla. I sensed that I always would be, just as I continued to mourn members of my family who had passed. But I knew I needed to keep going too, pressing through the mourning. I needed to keep fulfilling my calling for as many years as I had left. That's what she would have wanted. Still, everywhere I walked, I walked with a limp. This new limp was not caused by my little toe that always hurt. This new pain was a limp of my spirit, from the pain that filled my heart. I missed my friend. I truly missed her with all my being.

Back at home now there were Masses to celebrate and counseling sessions to lead. There were students, teachers, and parents to meet with at the school. There were weddings and funerals and baby baptisms and *quinceañeras*. There were retreats to lead and seminars with sessions for me to teach. There were people to talk to who simply needed a word of encouragement. There were people in the hospital to visit and pray for. There lay my calendar before me, with the scheduled responsibilities and of course, always the unscheduled needs that would fill in. Life kept going forward, and somehow that helped my grieving process. I kept moving.

I'd thought about this before, how my schedule can get pretty crazy, but I've never been one to slow down much. I get up at five most mornings and go hard until ten or eleven at night, and that's pretty much the way I like things. Why sit around when I'm still productive, still helpful, still able to do what I'm called to do?

Just this past weekend, we held a parish fiesta that ran from Friday evening until Sunday evening. I popped in and out all weekend long. Going on simultaneously at a retreat center was a marriage enrichment retreat (called Retrouvaille) for fifteen couples, and I helped give a few of the talks for that. On Friday night, Bishop Alemany High School held a baccalaureate for the senior class, and I was there for that, then I was there again for graduation on Saturday night. To top it off, I led two funerals and two weddings on Saturday. That was the fullness of my weekend. My life isn't always that busy. But a weekend like that isn't unusual.

I caught myself wondering once or twice during that weekend about that age-old question: Can a priest be married and still be successful in his role as a servant-leader? I'm sure he can, I concluded, but I know firsthand that if I'd been married, then I would not be able to do half of what I do today. I don't say that to ridicule married pastors or to disparage their calling. Not at all. We all have different callings in life, and my calling as a single man was plainly revealed to me many years ago. I'm content in that role today. I truly am.

Someone asked me last week if I'm ever going to retire. I said maybe, but not just yet. Priests are able to retire at age seventy and receive a pension and living quarters from the Church. As I write the last pages of this book, I'm now seventy-two and still going strong. I take one day off per week, usually a Monday, when I head up to the cabin and relax or do a few repairs. There I really feel away from the rush of city life. Or I'll visit my brothers and sisters and their families. Or just take a drive somewhere. I love going up to Fillmore, where I ministered for several years. The air cools slightly and the buildings of Los Angeles give way to the orange groves near Ventura County. It was one of my favorite ministry locations, and as I drive along I think, "This is heaven for me now. I loved living out here." As I drive I remember the various people and families in so many places I ministered to. I think about how I did a specific person's wedding or baptized his or her kids. These days I'm doing the weddings of the children I baptized and the children of couples I married years ago.

The ministry at Bishop Alemany continues to go well. Each day I find myself talking to students, counseling them, offering advice, encouraging them, praying with them. I continue to greet them in the mornings and go to their games and plays to cheer them on. I continue to lead retreats, and I continue to tell the story of Shayla.

Whenever I walk anywhere in the school, I give high fives to students. I think it's become a bit of a trademark with me. A few years back, on the fortieth anniversary of my becoming a priest, more than sixteen hundred students lined the sidewalks around the school, just to say thanks to me for being there. I walked through the middle of them, giving high fives to the entire student population. It was a fun day for me, and a tremendous honor to receive, but my aging hands were sure sore at the end. Later at the cathedral, I was awarded the Archdiocesan Youth Ministry Award for excellence in service. I've seen more and more these days just how much God has blessed me and the ministry in which I've been involved with Him over the years.

I continue to be active in leading marriage retreats through the diocese. I base much of what I know about love from my interaction with Shayla through the years.

My ministry has gone international. Several years back, I got involved with a call-in radio program for youth. That's still going today. It also led to a television ministry where I celebrate Mass on a Spanish-speaking television program that gets shown all over the world. I'm on TV two to five times a month. It seems funny to say it and is a continual surprise to me when I think about it, but I'm known in Spain, Mexico, South America, Central America, and throughout the states. People will stop me on the streets and say, "Hey, aren't you that guy I see on TV?"

The ministry is seldom easy. Never has been. Never will be. At times, it continues to be downright dangerous. For instance, a year or so ago I served as a chaplain aboard a ship bound for the Caribbean. There was an older couple onboard, and the wife fell very ill. I prayed for her healing and anointed her forehead and hands with oil, but the next day she died. Her husband, a war veteran, had been drinking this whole time as a way to escape his pain. He went on a rampage and threatened to kill everybody aboard ship. The captain called me to intervene.

Nothing within me wanted to intervene. Yet all those lessons kicked in, all the ones I'd learned over the years. Stay calm. Don't panic. Keep moving forward. Bathe everything in prayer. I went into the ship's hospital room and began to talk to him. He began pouring out his heart, and I simply listened to him for a long while. Sure, I was scared, and so I took hold of the man's hands as he talked and held them as calmly and reassuringly as I could.

In the end, after about an hour, we prayed together one last time. The man said he was tired, and so he lay down and went to sleep. The crisis was averted and no one was hurt. At the next port, the ship's administration called the authorities, and I never learned what happened to the man after that. But at least he didn't carry through with his terrible threats. I credit Shayla with developing within me many of those skills—how to listen and ask the right questions. How to care for people without stopping to inquire whether they are worthy or not.

Someone asked me just last week, what's next? And I answered simply that I want to keep doing exactly what I'm doing for as long as I'm able. I want to stay active at the school and the parish. I want to keep ministering to people. The parish is fine with that. The archdiocese said that my work with youth for all these years is inspiring younger priests to look at youth work as a lifelong calling, which I felt happy about. A while back, I asked the school principal what he and his staff thought of the plan for me to stay at Bishop Alemany longer, and he answered emphatically, "We want to keep you here as long as we can!"

And so I keep going. That's what I do.

Limping, I continue on.

CHAPTER 15

The Last Gift

STUDYING FOR A TALK A FEW DAYS AGO, I reviewed how the Hebrew word for love, *ahava*, has little to do with what one feels. I'd studied this concept before, but this time the knowledge stopped me cold. The word *ahava* actually means "I give." The idea is that when you love someone, you give to them. Love must be active, much more so than emotional. Shayla and I also liked the Greek word *agape*, which denotes an unconditional love, a love freely given, even if nothing is ever received back.

I smiled when I studied this, because I thought of the last gift Shayla ever gave to me. It was a gift that kept me going in the right direction. A gift that reminds me always of her love.

🌿 🌿 🌿

A few weeks after Shayla's death, the winter weather hung lifeless and rainy, even in Los Angeles. Dave called me on the phone one evening, and I heard warmth in his voice.

"Norm," he said, "I've still got this car of Shayla's and I don't quite know what to do with it. I've got my Jeep, so I don't need another vehicle." Here he paused for a moment, cleared his throat, then continued, "I'm wondering if you'd like to have it."

A smile tugged on the corners of my mouth. "I'd be honored," I said. "That would be a wonderful thing. You sure you don't need it?"

"Nah," he said. "It's something I'm pretty sure Shayla would want you to have."

We made a few other plans. Dave had some business in Los Angeles, so he'd drive the car down, visit some relatives and old friends while here, then take a plane back to Washington.

When I got off the phone, I felt glowing in the largeness of this gift. A car was a car, but this was more than just a car. Shayla's Lincoln was an extension of her personality. It had always been her dream car, a big tank of a car, the type of car she felt safest in. The image came to mind again, the one where she described to me how one last act of resolution would indeed happen, but it wouldn't be something that I would do for her. It would happen the other way around. She would give a tribute to me, not me to her. This car was it. This was Shayla's last way of saying good-bye.

Sure enough, a short time later Dave drove the Lincoln down from Washington. He arrived at my front door late one afternoon and honked the horn. Shayla's Lincoln was everything I remembered it to be. Fifteen years had passed since it first saw a showroom, but it hardly showed its age. It was cream colored and had power windows and locks and bench seats and a CD player and cushioned everything. We drove it to the DMV and transferred the papers over. Down the freeways of Los Angeles, this car flies as free as a flag.

Dave had some time still in Los Angeles, so we climbed into the Lincoln that same day and took a short road trip together. I drove him up to the cabin on Pine Mountain, the cabin he had designed years earlier for me and my friends. Although he'd drawn up the blueprints for the place, he'd never actually visited the site, and as I showed him around, he was quite impressed at its beauty and natural physicality. The land was still quiet, still crowded in all the best ways with bushy stands of pine and oak trees and a stream running in front. He could see it was a place of solitude and rest, of healing from the ills of daily life. It was a place where balm was spread on the wounds of the spirit. We two brothers soaked it in.

🌿 🌿 🌿

Heading back down from the mountain, Dave and I drove for some time without either of us saying anything. Spring was coming soon, and I had the driver's side window rolled down a bit. We moved slowly enough that we could hear birds singing outside. We were both alone with our thoughts.

I considered how Dave had been the true love of Shayla's life. I didn't doubt that. He had been her husband, her protector, her provider, the father of her children, her lifelong companion, her deepest friend. I wondered if I should say something to him about that, to kind of affirm it to him, but then I thought, no, he already knows that truth as firmly as hardened steel. Why say something when he can already feel it deep in his bones? The mere words I could offer wouldn't bring anything more than the concrete truth he already knew so deeply. Somehow it felt like words would be a clutter. And so we drove on in comfortable silence.

Me? How would I remember my love with Shayla? Simply put: I had loved Shayla in the Hebrew sense of the word. *Ahava*. In the Greek sense of the word. *Agape*. Ours had been a love that embodied giving. A love that gave freely, even if nothing was ever given back. I gave to her. And she gave to me. I'd recently spoken at an event attended by more than fifteen thousand youth. For a naturally shy person such as me, I never could have done that without Shayla's friendship worked into my makeup. Without her blessing. Without her coaching. Without her security. God had brought this woman to me to help me become who I am.

As the miles rolled on, Dave and I reached the outskirts of the city again. The air seemed clearer, and I thought back to that morning in February 1967 when I'd first met Shayla. How lucky, how fortuitous, some would say, that at a conference where two thousand people attended, I happened to go to the very seminar where Shayla was. I wasn't initially even planning to go to that seminar. It was only through Danny's insistence that I went. Such a set of blessed circumstances.

I remembered how Shayla introduced herself to me by her first name only, and how she spoke with a warm, direct voice, and how she approached me afterward saying, "Boy, you sure are a good listener."

I still could picture her back then, still so clearly in my mind's eye. I could see her soap-scrubbed complexion, her dark hair cut to her shoulders. Her eyes, blue and piercing, and the way her eyebrows mischievously arched whenever she smiled. That day when Shayla and I first met was one of the most wonderful days of my life. I knew it only in hindsight, and yet I knew it with no shadow of doubt.

Images blended into one another in my mind's eye as we drove, and I could see years stretch out like sunlight on the horizon. I could see Shayla and me that night when we chaperoned the junior high dance. I could see us walking among the evening-time classrooms, talking so freely as we walked, and I saw us at her favorite place along the cliffs of Palos Verdes, me wondering if Danny was going to be upset.

I remembered the first time Shayla and I had kissed. How it made me feel loved by her. I remembered our hikes through the woods. Our many conversations over burgers and fries. Our work on the retreats, and me watching her out of the corner of my eye.

I recalled our one key conversation, the day when I dropped her off at the airport when I first knew I was in love with her, and she with me. How a month later we talked about the possibility of marriage. How the words slipped out of our mouths with such force and power that they could never be returned.

I remembered how we considered the future together. How we prayed for guidance. How Shayla was sure that God was telling her that I would be the father of many families. How that had come to pass in the many years since.

I saw my ordination. I saw Shayla begin to go on dates again. I saw myself presiding over the marriage ceremony of Dave and Shayla. I saw myself baptizing their children. I saw myself visiting their home so many times. I saw phone calls, and dinners around their table, and so many moments of laughter in their living room.

I saw me performing the wedding ceremonies of their children. I saw me baptizing Dave and Shayla's grandchildren.

I saw both Shayla and me growing old. I saw us both battling cancer. I saw myself at her bedside when she was so sick. I could remember the exact sound of her voice. Her voice was still with me. Always with me.

I saw myself officiating at Shayla's funeral.

All those years, they stretched forward and backward, and now, here I was, side by side with Dave, and we were driving in Shayla's car. And Shayla was in heaven in a city of gold. She was cancer free and experiencing all the wonder and light of new creation. She was laughing and singing with friends and family members who'd preceded her there. Through that heavenly city ran a river of the water of life, bright as crystal, flowing from the throne of God and of the Lamb through the middle of the streets of that city. On either side of the river were fruit trees for the healing of the nations. There was no sorrow of Shayla's that heaven could not heal. She was looking down on both of us as we drove in her Lincoln, I knew, and she was saying, "There is my husband, the love of my life. And there is the man I called my close friend, the man who now drives my car."

No, it was not luck that brought Shayla and me together. It was not chance. There in the car, I thought about the intricate relationship I had with Shayla, how God wove the threads of our lives together in ways I could have never imagined. The events that I looked back on seemed so disconnected at the times they occurred, but now they all looked so much more linear, so much more joined by an all-knowing outstretched Hand. I thought back to when I was a child, how painfully shy I was, and how God brought so many people and events together to help shape and mold me. Shayla led the pack in that regard. God used Shayla to help me learn to reach out to people, to love them, to care for them always as God wanted me to.

We reached our destination, and I dropped Dave off. He was going to go see Shayla's sister Marge. We said our good-byes, and I thanked him again for the car. He said not to mention it. We shook hands. Then we gave each other a quick, manly hug and slapped each other on the back. We'd call each other soon.

And then I was alone.

Just me and the Lincoln, and the sense of Shayla's presence in her car.

As I pulled away from the curb and headed back to the parish, I thought about how these good times in our lives, these challenging times, these times of mourning even, they are all allowed by God for a reason. God is not absent through any of them. If we stop and look we can see God with us. He works with us. He guides us.

Always, always we journey with God. It's the way of devotion we must travel. It's the way of giving we must drive. The Shepherd is our Light, and He guides us over rough roads and through dark storms and around corners where the road beyond lies unseen.

About the Author

NORM SUPANCHECK was born in 1942 and grew up in Long Beach, California. He's spent his life devoted to serving God and helping people.

An ordained priest for the Archdiocese of Los Angeles since 1968, Father Norm's current assignment is chaplain at Alemany High School in Mission Hill, California, a position he has held since 2002.

Father Norm leads various marriage enrichment programs through the Catholic Church, including Retrouvaille, Marriage Encounter, and Engaged Encounter. He works with many youth training programs and is actively involved in a variety of community service organizations.

Proficient in Spanish, Father Norm celebrates Mass in Spanish up to five times a month on El Sembrador TV Station (ESNE), which is broadcast worldwide.

He holds a bachelor's degree in philosophy from Saint John's Seminary and a master's degree in applied theology from Graduate Theological Union.

About the Collaborative Author

MARCUS BROTHERTON is a journalist and professional writer known internationally for his books and literary collaborations with high-profile public figures, humanitarians, inspirational leaders, and military personnel.

He has authored or coauthored more than twenty-five books, including the widely acclaimed *Feast For Thieves*, the much-loved *Finding Martha's Place*, and *We Who Are Alive and Remain*, a *New York Times* bestseller.

SI 10-8-15

OS 12-10-15

AC 2-8-16

AC 4-11-16

ET 6-13-16

WH 7-25-16

OA 9-26-16

TC 11-28-16

TC 12-1-16 KP

This is me when I was a year old. People say I was a cute baby. I'm not sure.

My parents, Tony and Alice, with dreams of a family

Me in elementary school

Me in seventh grade

Shayla as a young girl in Texas

When I was a young cowboy

Jim, John, and me in front of Signal Hill Sheet Metal

Our third rocket—
ready to launch!

Shayla swimming
at Catalina Island

I would like to thank you for helping me to become a priest. A man does not become a priest by himself, but by the efforts of many people. You in your way have helped to bring me to the priesthood. For this I will always be grateful.

I am now *your* priest. Please continue helping me, especially by your prayers, that I may be able to serve you and the rest of the people of God.

Your priest,
Norm

My ordination card, 1968

Me, the new priest, in 1968

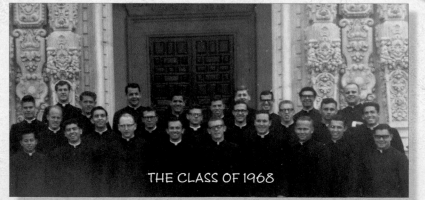

THE CLASS OF 1968

My chalice,
handmade by my fami

Shayla, always radiant

Dave and Shayla with their
first baby, godmother
Eileen, and me

Shayla and Dave
on their wedding day

Shayla with Dave,
the love of her life.

Dave and Shayla and their daughters

The cabin we built,
designed by Dave.
Ebner

Me around 1973

Leading a parade in East L.A., 1979

Campus ministry, mid-1980s

In traction after my motorcycle accident

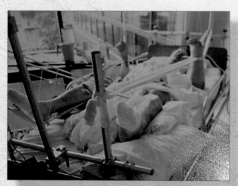

Enjoying a laugh, four months after the accident

Meeting Pope John Paul, 1991

Giving high-fives at Bishop Alemany School to celebrate my 45th anniversary in the ministry

Shayla and me, toward the end

DISCARD